# AND YET I LIVE

A Play in Three Acts and a Prologue

by

VERA I. ARLETT

NEW PLAYWRIGHTS' NETWORK

First Published March 1976.

AND YET I LIVE

STAGE PLAN

49044153X

## CHARACTERS

WILLIAM . . . . . . . . . . . . . . . . . . . . . . . . . . . Earl of Ware

BERTRAM . . . . . . . . . . . . . . . . . . . . . . . his half brother

PHILIP . . . . . . . . . . . . . . . . . . . . . . . his nephew and heir

CLEMENT. . . . . . . . . . . . . . . . . . . . formerly a Lay Brother

HUGH. . . . . . . . . . . . . . . . . . . . . . . . . . . . .a serving man

JOAN . . . . . . . . . . . . . . . . . . . . . . . . . . . . . .wife to Philip

MARGARET . . . . . . . her waiting woman, and sister to Bertram

The poem quoted in Act One is an anonymous lyric, contemporary with the action of the play.

AND YET I LIVE
Setting designed by Harald Melvill.
The lighting plot is also his and his help in technical matters is gratefully acknowledged.

| ACT I | PROLOGUE |
| Scene 1. | (Eight years later.) |
| Scene 2. | (Six weeks later.) |
| ACT II | (A few weeks later.) |
| ACT III | (Several months later.) |

The whole action takes place in the Hall of the hereditary Castle of the Earl of Ware, in the North of England.

Time                          From 1529 onwards

# AND YET I LIVE

## PROPERTY PLOT

### Prologue (On Stage)

Handsome, richly coloured Tapestry, on Wall up R. (This covers
secret panel in the panelled wall.)
Cushioned covering for window-seat up L.
Several handsomely bound books to dress the stage. Books,
sheets of music and poetry on table, or bench — but usually
on or near window-seat.
Candles (which should vary in height from scene to scene) in
various parts of the room.
These are permanent props, and with the exception of the
tapestry and window-seat cushion, vary in position from scene
to scene. A tall, ecclesiastical type candle, in a high ornamental
stand, up L.
A large book, in a white leather binding ('Philip')
Lady's handkerchief — possibly with narrow lace border 'Philip'
Small square of parchment, with writing on it, and a small lock
of yellow hair attached to it by a silken thread (Philip)
Ornamental crucifix on wall down R.

### (OFF STAGE)

Two bracket stands with lighted candles (Hugh off stage R.)
Taper (Hugh)
Cloak, hat, gloves and riding boots (Bertram...personal props)
Glass Crash — Effect off stage up R.
Clash of steel on steel — duelling effect off stage up R.
NOTE: Window L.C. should have small section that opens
(inwards) on a catch.

### ACT I. Scene I

Several books to dress stage...with other books, music sheets
and collections of poems etc., on window-seat, and on floor
near it.
Embroidery (Joan)
Sewing (Margaret)
2 bags of silk thread etc., (Joan and Margaret)

### ACT I. Scene II

Pewter plate, with a leg of cold chicken — a hunk of brown

bread and a lettuce leaf, and a goblet of wine — all on a wooden tray (Bertram…Off R.)
Bunch of keys (Bertram — personal prop)

## ACT II

Needlework (Joan)
Workbag (Joan)
Small square of parchment, with writing on it, and a small lock of yellow hair attached to it by a silken thread (Joan…It is in her workbag)
Cloak (Philip…over back of a chair, on stage)
Small dagger (Joan…personal prop)

## ACT III

2 small glass phials, each with a differently coloured liquid inside. (Clement personal prop)
Work-bag with silks and threads, and a small square of parchment with writing on it, and a small lock of yellow hair attached to it by a silken thread. (Joan personal prop)
NOTE. (As this piece of parchment keeps turning up in various places, it might be as well to have several identical pieces standing by, and always to check on them before the curtain rise… especially as it is destroyed in Act III)
Rosary (Clement…personal prop)
Small packet of Songs and Poems of Old Provence (on window seat up L.)
Flagon of wine — goblet — earthenwear ewer of water and a small hand-towel, all on a wooden tray, off R. (Margaret)

## "AND YET I LIVE"

## PROLOGUE

The Scene is laid in the hall of the hereditary castle of the Earls of Ware. It is spacious and well proportioned, with a large window up left deeply recessed behind a Gothic arch, which gives it an ecclesiastical beauty. There is a stone window-seat, which is comfortably cushioned. There is also a much smaller window, which is recessed, and is L.C. of the back wall. This window has a small section that can be opened by a catch, and is used by 'Bertram' for the business of throwing out the handkerchief, during the Prologue.

Below the main window, there is a large open fireplace, with a 'hood' above it, on which is carved the Arms of the Earls of Ware. A raised hearth-stone juts into the hall, with on it a trivet for the burning of logs.

On the right the walls are panelled up to about two-thirds of their height......roughly about 8' with a recessed arched door D.S.R. On the narrow section of wall, at right angles to the door, hangs an ornamental crucifix.

On the section of panelled wall up R, there is a secret door
(or sliding panel, worked by a spring) that conceals a 'Priests
Hole'. The greater part of this wall is further masked by a large
handsome and colourful tapestry, which the present Earl of Ware
has brought back from his travels abroad.

The main portion of the back wall contains a raised corridor,
which runs behind four pillars, supporting Gothic arches above.
The L.C. arch is wider than the other two, and serves as the
entrance to the hall, and one or two shallow stone steps give
access to the lower level. This corridor, which leads off to R. is
backed by a plain stone wall – on which the shadows of the
two duelists are thrown, at the end of the prologue. The window
through which 'Bertram' falls in the prologue, and 'Joan' jumps
at the end of Act III is off R. and is not visible to the audience.

A plain trestle table stands in front of the tapestry panel,
with an 'X' arm-chair above, and a plain stool below it, and a
second stool at the side, if desired. A small monks' chest or
bench stands in front of the corridor pillars, on which the lighted
candles brought on by 'Hugh' can be placed. A stool stands near
the smaller of the two windows, on which is stood the one tall
candle, in its candlestick (prologue) another stool stands above
the fireplace.

NOTES:
This scenic description can, of course, be simplified and
altered to suit available conditions. The pillars, for instance, need
only be 'half-rounds' as only half of each is visible. The corridor
rostrum can be of any height and width, or may be omitted,
if desired, together with the steps.

Gothic arches should be used if and where possible – but any
other 'period' can be used, except 'Tudor', which would make
the Castle too contemporary – or they may be omitted alto-
gether. The smaller window can be left out, as may be the 'hood'
from the fire. All arches or openings should be 'revealed', in
order to give the illusion of 'thickness' to the walls.

If the opening to the Priest's Hole is placed at the upper side of the panel, and opens inwards or slides downstage, the 'business' can be masked by the manner in which the tapestry is held back, the main purpose of the exercise being for 'Philip' to disappear into the wall.

The present Earl has travelled widely, and the curtains and hangings show a colour and richness somewhat rare in these home fastnesses of the English nobility; there are also many books about, for he is a great reader, and patron of the art of printing.

It is Autumn, 1529. King Henry VIII is on the throne, ruling despotically, but there is unrest all round.

The Earl has not long been married to a foreign bride; his younger brother, now dead, also looked further than home, and chose his bride in Provence. These facts are not acceptable to the English yeomen and tenantry.

When the curtain rises, the Hall is dark, except for a pool of light given by one candle, set in a tall candlestick of beautiful design. The flame glows and flickers.

BERTRAM, the Earl's half-brother, enters right and crosses the Hall, having just come in from riding, in heavy boots and cloak. He is about forty, well set-up, and obviously a soldier. Close to the window seat, he stumbles against someone, and gives an exclamation of surprise and annoyance. It is PHILIP, the Earl's young nephew and heir. He has been reading, sitting on the ground, his head resting on the window-seat, when the foggy darkness fell. He did not call for more lights, but brooded in the twilight, the large book he had been reading left on the ground beside him.

BERTRAM: Must you lurk in the shadows? Mother of God, who are you? Are you one of the hosts of darkness that you fear the light? (claps hands and calls loudly) Hugh, lights here! (HUGH, a serving man, enters quickly and lights up several other candles and retires).

BERTRAM: (as soon as there is light enough to discern the object of his scorn) Oh! It's you. Pardon my lord. (This is *rather perfunctory)* I didn't recognise you. But then, I've no cat's eyes to see in the dark. I hope my riding boots didn't deal unkindly with your ribs?

PHILIP: *(still sitting rather huddled up, with his knees drawn up to his chin)* It's no matter if they did.

BERTRAM: No matter! You're becoming something of a philosopher, young sir. And I suppose that's the next best thing for those who won't turn soldier. *(Turns away, with a touch of involuntary contempt)*

PHILIP: Is it? Then I must disappoint you on both counts. For at the moment I am incapable of philosophy. *(While Bertram's back is turned he slips some small thing he has held hidden in his hand between the leaves of the book, which is on the ground. Bertram is busy pulling off his heavy riding gloves).* I have failed to make my peace with sorrow.

BERTRAM: *(Turning sharply)* What's that? And you so lately home! You would not be vagrant again, and you my lord's own nephew and his heir! Fie, sir. Your place is here.

PHILIP: I'm only the younger son of a younger son. It can't matter much what I do, can it?

BERTRAM: It has pleased heaven to remove your father and your elder brother; and now you will — or may — inherit all. You should do nothing inconsistent with the dignity of the house.

PHILIP: *(Getting up and stretching, like an animal in a cage)* Oh, the dignity of the house! It weighs me down. It stifles me. I must soon be on my travels again. I'll turn soldier of fortune and sell my swordsmanship to the King of France, or some pleasure-loving Italian Duke. Isn't that a plan after your own heart?

BERTRAM: No sir.

PHILIP: No?

BERTRAM: No. There's fighting to be done at home, often enough. Why not use your sword in our own King Henry's service? There's always the Scots Border. Plenty to do up there when they break out. And you wouldn't have to wait very long. It isn't healthy when they keep us quiet as they've been these last months, though I doubt now whether there will be much to do before Spring.

PHILIP: I believe the climate is vile. And I suppose you couldn't understand that I should hate harrying the Scots?

BERTRAM: No, sir.

PHILIP: Now isn't that strange?

BERTRAM: Most strange to me. I deplore the mixture of alien blood in you. Our good lords should marry honest English wives, not these foreign women. Both our present lord, *and* his brother! It's too much.

PHILIP: It is indeed........You don't care for foreigners, do you Bertram?

BERTRAM: No, sir.

PHILIP: Why not?

BERTRAM: They aren't English.

PHILIP: How simple! So, can't you see, that being half a foreigner myself, I'm not the least interested as to where, exactly, the English and the Scots fix their Border. They could blot it out for all I care.

BERTRAM: That shall never happen! Of course there will always be a Border! How else will you keep out the Scots?

PHILIP: I hadn't thought........

BERTRAM: That's just it. You don't know, you don't trouble to think of these things. Let me tell you, it would be very different if you lived in the Border country. You'd think then, when you had your cattle and your women stolen —

PHILIP: *(reprovingly)* Oh, Bertram! And you talk of Italy! Ttt...

BERTRAM: What have I said now?

PHILIP: You should put the women first, Bertram, and the cattle afterwards. Italians would do that instinctively, you know. Besides, women appreciate a little compliment now and then.

BERTRAM: Your tongue's too glib, young sir. I only wish you were as handy with your sword.

PHILIP: Oh, I'm handy enough when roused,

BERTRAM: In that case, I still fail to see what's wrong with the Border.

PHILIP: I'm not interested. Besides, you can't expect me to live in a perpetual east wind, or a downpour.

BERTRAM: *(seething with contempt)* Yet you offered to sell your sword to the King of France, or an Italian Duke!

PHILIP: Oh, they're civilised. Since I represent a noble house — however unworthily — I should not be expected to fight

unless I felt inclined. And that wouldn't be too often. Besides,
I don't want to go to uncouth places I want to go back — to
Italy; or to that little estate I have in Provence — you wouldn't
believe what spring is like — in Provence.

BERTRAM: I should think your Uncle's experiences abroad
would have cured you of seeking adventures there. Isn't
he warning enough?

PHILIP:Ah, yes. He is a man of dark doom, my Uncle. You can
see it in his face, can't you? In his eyes? They're hurt and
brooding. You know what they did to him once?

BERTRAM: *(slowly, as if he has never spoken of it before)*
I believe they tortured him. It is a rumour.

PHILIP: It is true. He cannot speak of it, and no-one will risk
my lord's enmity by saying anything to him.

BERTRAM: I wish the truth could be known. He lives like a
hermit, brooding and mysterious among his books. He is so
rarely seen abroad that he has become more of a legend than
a man. He used not to be so when he was young.

PHILIP: Like me, he loves the South and Italy. And he stayed
away too long.

BERTRAM: Yes, he was abroad too many years; I know he was
in Rome when the Emperor's troops laid siege to the city.

PHILIP: But when the city fell, there was a three days' riot of
butchery and pillage. It was then they took him. He was
imprisoned for some weeks and when he came out, he was
as we know him now.

BERTRAM: A strange, marked man.

PHILIP: He seems always to be looking for his own fate. And
that is hidden away in the shadows.

BERTRAM: Heaven forbid! And he but one year married to so
young a lady! They should have children, and a quiet age.
He should return to life now.

PHILIP: *(Turning away)* The arms of this house, Bertram, should
be a bat rampant — a withered bough — and a background of
night. No stars, mark you; no moonbeams, or hopeful silvery
nonsense of that sort. *(Spinning round again and facing
Bertram)* Well? You look reproving. But you don't contra-
dict . . . . because you can't.

BERTRAM: Sir — *(He looks a little helplessly round the room
and his eye catches the tall candlestick)* Even you — though

you sat and brooded like a shadow among the shadows — even you had a single light. There is a world of difference between an unlighted room, and that which shows but one tall candle in the dark.

PHILIP: Yes, yes. Have you ever realised, Bertram, that my uncle's mind is like a dark room — with only one light in it? And that is —

BERTRAM: The Lady Nicola. I know.

PHILIP: Bertram, you and I should change places.

BERTRAM: That would be against the will of God.

PHILIP: He has given you, then, a bar sinister, and me a clean shield. Well? Was it also His will that your mother was beautiful, and the old Earl lusty in his youth?

BERTRAM: Sir —

PHILIP: I would say it was all in the day's work, as far as honest human nature goes. Oh, you've no thought, no dream, no ambition outside this house! You live for it. If need be, you would die for it.

BERTRAM: I trust so, as God hears me.

PHILIP: So there you are. I wouldn't. And I'm next in the line of succession — in which line you can never be. This house, these treasures, these lands — my uncle's place at Court — all these should be yours.

BERTRAM: *(Emphatically)* No! I say no!

PHILIP: And I say yes, if there were justice and good common sense in the ordering of the world. But there is not.

BERTRAM: I beseech you, sir, do not repeat foreign heresies here! I know you're a travelled man, and I've never left my own land. But we keep the Faith at home — and let the profligate Italians and the unbelieving French talk themselves crazy, if they want to! Yes! And the Reformers Too! We *know* God is on His throne for ever, and Our Lady stands beside Him in eternal intercession for us!

PHILIP: *(Pensively)* Does she now? It's a pretty thought . . . . . .

BERTRAM: Sir, I implore you . . . . . .

PHILIP: Among the very many things I can't understand, Bertram, is why soldiers are always so extraordinarily pious. You go about hacking and hewing, and running people through on the slightest provocation, and yet you're always the first to turn round and talk of God's love and kindness and mercy. Doesn't it ever strike you as a little inconsistent?

BERTRAM: No. I perceive no inconsistency, sir.

PHILIP: Really?

BERTRAM: Orders are to be obeyed, not discussed, whether they are God's, or man's.

PHILIP: How discouraging you can be, Bertram. Now I, who pore over my books like a poor scholar; I, who write long hours as though I were a Lay Brother or a sober historian; I, who cannot bear to see even an ox pole-axed — *(Spreads his hands in an expressive gesture)*

BERTRAM: *(Expectantly)* Yes?

PHILIP: *(With sudden intensity)* — I think something has gone badly wrong, either with God or man. But I don't know which. *(Turns and stares out of the window).*

BERTRAM: *(Striding up to him, and gripping his shoulder)* Take care! There's an ugly doom waiting for those who betray the Faith these days — the Faith as King Henry sees it. Haven't you noticed that he's in no mood to show mercy now?

PHILIP: *(almost savagely)* I've noticed that he grows daily more like God . . . . .
*(Bertram, with an exclamation of horror, claps his hand on his sword)*

PHILIP: *(Spinning round and repulsing Bertram with a dainty gesture)* . . . In his own estimation only. *(He has resumed an airy bantering tone with this remark)* Good Bertram, you can have little or no pleasure in my company or conversation. Why don't you go?

BERTRAM: I'm going — and gladly. *(Strides to exit, where he turns)* I wish to heaven you had favoured your father, instead of your mother.

PHILIP: *(angry)* Now that won't do at all, Bertram. I know my mother was a foreigner to you, and my own heart turns to the South. My tastes are more foreign than English, and I'm an exile here. But when it comes to talking of fathers and mothers —

BERTRAM: *You* can retaliate. Your pardon sir. In one sense, I also am an exile.

PHILIP: Oh, it's as I said. You should be the heir, not I. You should have the doubtful privilege of living and dying for the House of Ware —

BERTRAM: I ask no better fate.

PHILIP: *(Clutching his head)* God! What a mind!

BERTRAM: It is a single one.

PHILIP: It is indeed. You — with your village cousins — will never bring disgrace on us. That'll probably be *my* contribution to the family history!

BERTRAM: It would kill your uncle —

PHILIP: Oh, I wish I could forget him! His dark, tragic face haunts me — day and night. I can find no peace here — He's a tortured man.

BERTRAM: Careful —

(WARE *enters. He hardly acknowledges their salutations).*

WARE: Where is Nicola?

PHILIP: Isn't she in her own apartments?

WARE: No.

BERTRAM: My Lady was walking in the garden about an hour ago — just at sunset. Perhaps she is not yet indoors.

WARE: She should not do that! These autumn evenings are cold and treacherous. There's a mist rising now, and most likely it'll turn to a ground frost later on.

BERTRAM: I'll go out into the gardens again and take a look at the avenue as well. She walks there sometimes *(Exits)*

PHILIP: I expect she's safely in her room all the time.

WARE: No — no, she is not *(Paces restlessly)* I'm anxious about her, Philip.

PHILIP: Oh, why?

WARE: In spite of all my care, she seems — how can I explain what I feel about her? She almost seems to be eluding life.

PHILIP: *(Dryly)* She is not ill, you know.

WARE: *(Hastily)* No, no, of course she isn't, I did not say she was. But there are times when I almost feel she is on the far side of the parting of body and soul. It is as if her hands were too small to hold the gift of life. It's too strong, too rough a thing for her to grasp. She might so easily let it slip —

PHILIP: *(Matter of fact)* Yellow-haired girls always look frail and other worldly. It's a habit of theirs, and they use it, — for their own advantage. Sheer illusion, uncle. They're just the same flesh and blood as other women in the end.

WARE: You've become singularly matter of fact for a poet

and scholar! I always thought they were fanciful where women were concerned, especially beautiful women.

PHILIP: Beautiful women are best left in poems.

WARE: *(Unheeding and pacing again restlessly)* The dark has come down early this afternoon .... perhaps I made a mistake to bring Nicola to these low-lying misty lands. I'd like to get her away. She's used to mountains, and clear air.

PHILIP: . . . . . . And the South. I belong there — to Provence, to Italy and the countries where there's sun. I fear the wind is at my heels again.

WARE: Oh, you! You come and go, like a thought in the brain; but I wish you belonged *here*, as Bertram does, I can trust him like *(touching one of the supporting columns)* like one of these. He helps support the house. Heaven knows what I should do without him!

PHILIP: You won't have to do without him at present. I gather that peace has just broken out on the Border.

WARE: Don't be frivolous, Philip. You've never seen a Border raid.

PHILIP: My *dear* uncle! You know I like to dissociate myself from the cruder pastimes of mankind.

WARE: You're obviously in the wrong country, and with the wrong people.

PHILIP: Poisoning always seems to me a much more refined way of getting rid of one's enemies than slashing them about with knives. Crude, as I remarked.

WARE: I deplore your interest in drugs, especially the dangerous kind.

PHILIP: I fear you would deplore many of my interests — if you knew what they are. So, on the whole, you don't object to my going on my travels again?

WARE: You'll go, whether I object or not. So why waste words? Times are dangerous, but I know you're able and willing to look after yourself. And when I die, I've no doubt you'll suddenly be discovered, near at hand, all ready to inherit.

PHILIP: *(Looking away)* A son should do that.

WARE: Should, but never will.

PHILIP: But it is the fervent hope of us all —

WARE: A hope — *(Shrugs and changes abruptly)* Another year
I must try and take Nicola somewhere warmer. She's ailing,
Philip. Even London would be better than this. But I've left
it too late in the year to travel now.

*(Enter MARGARET hurriedly, followed by BERTRAM)*

MARGARET: My Lord, she's in the Chapel. I fear she's faint.
Will you come?

WARE: *(Anxiously)* She's not ill, is she?

MARGARET: No, my Lord, only a little faint. She asked me to
fetch you. I think she had gone there to pray, and lost her
senses for a few moments. Luckily I went there too, it being
St. Martin's Day, and my own boy called Martin, as you know.
He would have been   eighteen this birthday, my Lord, had he
lived. But to die so young —

WARE: There's no need to weep for that, Margaret.

*(He cuts short further reminiscences and hurries out, followed
by MARGARET)*

BERTRAM: My lord is unnecessarily anxious! He thinks too
much about her.

PHILIP: Yes, yes.

*(He has been staring after his uncle in a dazed kind of way. He
takes a couple of steps forward, as though to follow, and falls
over the book still on the ground.)*

BERTRAM: The book you were reading before the shadows
fell! *(He picks it up and offers it to Philip, who has stumbled
against the window seat. Something falls out of the book —
BERTRAM does not hold it with the natural ease of a scholar.
Both men stop quickly to pick up the object. BERTRAM
retrieves it first, and examines it. It is a handkerchief with
which is folded a piece of yellow hair tied to parchment.
He steps back with an exclamation of horror and surprise.
He slips the parchment back in the book and holds up the
handkerchief.)*

BERTRAM: This belongs to the Lady Nicola!

PHILIP: *(Impudently)* Well?

BERTRAM: Well? You stole it, I suppose.

PHILIP: Thieving is not one of my habits.

BERTRAM: What! She didn't — give it to you? Take care,
young sir. We don't want any of your Italian manners here.
*(Instinctively his right hand feels for his sword.)*

PHILIP: *(angrily)* Give me that handkerchief! Give it to me, do you hear?

BERTRAM: It's not yours. I'll return it where it belongs.

PHILIP: That you won't! It's mine — it was given to me. Let me have it — or I'll come and take it. *(His hand is on his sword too)*

BERTRAM: She had no right to give it to you. You can't trust these foreign women and now we've got one here to play fast and loose with my Lord's honour in his very house.

PHILIP: *(whipping out his sword)* How dare you criticise her! How dare you say she had no right! Who are you to speak of her like that?

BERTRAM: A truer branch of this good tree than you or my Lady are showing yourselves.

PHILIP: *(advancing)* Give me that handkerchief, or I'll make you.

BERTRAM: *(parrying)* No! I'll not fight my Lord's heir! And you can find your treasure by daylight, if you want to. It will be well sodden by then.

*(He has backed to within easy distance of one of the windows. Without taking his eyes off his opponent, he drops the handkerchief through with his left hand. PHILIP gives an exclamation of anger and disappointment.)*

PHILIP: I'll make you sorry for that, you interfering hound. *(Lunges)*

BERTRAM: I'm an older hand at this than you are, and a quicker one too. Put up your sword, for I swear I'll do nothing but defend myself.

PHILIP: And I swear I'll taunt you till you want to run me through!

BERTRAM: I do that already. There's no need to put me further in the mood.

PHILIP: To business then.

*(He makes for BERTRAM with grim determination.*

*BERTRAM backs skilfully till he reaches the arch, centre back. PHILIP pressing him hard. They go from sight along the corridor, but their conflicting shadows are thrown on the wall and the ring of steel on steel is still heard.)*

MARGARET *comes hurrying in from door down Right.*

MARGARET: Bertram, where are you? Come quickly — help —

*(Suddenly she sees the shadows and hears the sound of steel. She stands a moment, transfixed. Then there is a loud crash, a shriek, and silence. The shadows disappear. She covers her face with her hands for a moment, and gives a moan.)*

MARGARET: Jesu! Mary! No more, I beseech you! No more evil to this unhappy house! Stave off the peril and the doom — *(PHILIP comes in, white and haggard. He walks uncertainly and his sword is still unsheathed.)*

MARGARET: *(falling back, amazed and frightened)* What have you done?

PHILIP: *(dazed)* I.....I.....think I've killed Bertram. Yes..... I've killed Bertram.

MARGARET: You can't have killed him! You're demented. It isn't true.

PHILIP: We — fought. It was all my fault. He didn't want me to. But I meant to kill him — then. I saw red, and made him fight with me. And now —

MARGARET: *(with a moan)* Isn't there enough sorrow, but death must come twice in one night?

PHILIP: Twice?

MARGARET: *(sobbing)* Nicola —

PHILIP: I don't understand —

MARGARET: She went out on a little sigh. No pain, no agony, no smallest stain of suffering. She lay back in his arms and sighed once. That was all.

PHILIP: *(Still out of himself)* What are you telling me? None of this is true. It can't be. There's no sense in what you're saying, Margaret.

MARGARET: *(Realising that he is still dazed, goes to him and puts a hand on his arm)* You must understand. Nicola is dead. *(He makes no response. She repeats it again slowly and simply like teaching a child a lesson)* Nicola is dead.

PHILIP: *(with a hand to his head)* No — no. It isn't real. This is some terrible dream.....I shall wake up in a minute, and everything will be all right *(Laughing uncertainly)* I haven't killed Bertram. Nicola isn't dead. She was alive and warm an hour ago. She's still alive. She is.

MARGARET: *(shaking his arm)* No, no. She is not. Go to my Lord. He's nearly distracted. He'll all but die himself. He needs you. He's asking for you — and Bertram.

PHILIP: Bertram can't go...it's all a mistake. I never wanted to kill Bertram — at least only for a minute, because he said something about Nicola — Nicola. *(Sways, holding his shoulder, and stumbles to the window seat. MARGARET runs to him and feels the shoulder.)*

MARGARET: Blood....then you're wounded too.

PHILIP: It's nothing....nothing. Just a scratch.

MARGARET: Brother Clement will see to it for you. He's in the Chapel with my Lady. But she's past his aid now.

PHILIP: *(leaning against her slightly)* Oh, Margaret, Margaret! Things like this *don't* happen. We only dream them, when we're too unhappy for tears.

*(HUGH enters)*

HUGH: Father John is preparing the Chapel. He needs more candles.

MARGARET: Take what you will. Take them all if need be. Come Philip. *(Rises)*

*(HUGH takes all, except the one tall candle which was alight at the beginning of the play)*

PHILIP: I will come —

*(MARGARET walks slowly to the exit R. As she passes the cross that is hung on the wall, she pauses in front of it and bows her head.)*

MARGARET: God rest her, for she was a most sweet lady.... Nicola, gentle saint, pray for me when you reach your glory, for I am alone and I am afraid.

*(She goes out)*

PHILIP: *(Just audibly)* .......A most sweet lady *(He follows her)*

*(HUGH comes in again and removes the solitary candle.)*


CURTAIN

## "AND YET I LIVE"

### ACT 1

#### SCENE 1

*Eight years have elapsed since the Prologue. It is now spring, 1537.*

*The setting is the same, except that it is broad daylight and the sun streams in through the great windows.*

MARGARET, *looking distinctly older, sits at her needlework.*

JOAN, *a young and lovely girl of about sixteen, sits in the window embrasure. There are books beside her, and she often dips into them, obviously preferring reading to sewing.*

MARGARET: *(Gently recalling* JOAN's *attention from a book to needlework)* So, by this time next week, you will be a bride, my lady Joan!

JOAN: If God wills. *(Picks up her work without much enthusiasm.)*

MARGARET: He could not do otherwise. At last He has sent a blessing to this old house, and I thank Him I have lived long enough to see it.

JOAN: I suppose you were all wondering what I was like before Philip brought me home here, weren't you?

MARGARET: That's only human, isn't it?

JOAN: Am I anything like you all imagined me to be?

MARGARET: Much lovelier.

JOAN: Thank you.

MARGARET: It's a great event, the coming of a bride, when your husband is my lord's heir.

JOAN: *(thoughtfully letting her work fall)* Margaret, why doesn't *he* marry again.

MARGARET: *(uneasily)* That's my lord's own affair, not ours.... though we'd all have the greatest joy of it, if he did — even his nephew.

JOAN: Oh, Philip would be glad enough, I know. He's generous and kind....in a way. I mean, he doesn't want to keep everything in the inheritance for himself.

MARGARET: You've a fine fortune, to be loved and chosen by him! He's been a favourite, you know, here and abroad; and many a fine lady has cried her eyes out for him. He's been gay and cruelly thoughtless in his time, but that's all changed now, and so is he. You can't believe how different he is since he started coming here again.

JOAN: When was that, Margaret?

MARGARET: Oh last summer. He'd kept away from us for seven long years. He'd left us a flippant, impudent boy, fit to break your heart with his merciless tongue. He returned a man, with quietness and a sense of power in him.

JOAN: Why did he keep away from his uncle, all those years? *(*MARGARET *does not reply)* I mean, how *could* he? I think my lord is the greatest man I've ever met. He is so utterly unlike anyone I've ever seen.......but of course there isn't anyone like him, is there?

MARGARET: *(Dryly)* No, least of all, Philip.

JOAN: *(hastily picking up the neglected needlework again)* I haven't met many people, Margaret. My mother was ill for a long time, and she died when I was quite a child. My father and brothers never troubled about me much — so I was alone a great deal.

MARGARET: I can see you've run wild. No lady should be allowed to do that.

JOAN: No? Well, I admit my favourite society was dogs and horses — till Philip came.

MARGARET: No wonder you found him dazzling by comparison.

JOAN: He came first to see my father and brothers. They had endless talks about the king's policy and how wicked he was to pass that Act making himself out to be the Head of the Church.

MARGARET: Hush! These are dangerous times. You had best remember that questions of the king's policy are beyond your understanding. They've nothing to do with you.

JOAN: But they have! That's why I'm here. My father and brothers are more and more involved in some secret business in the North. Philip is in it too. Our house is empty except for a few old servants, so I have to be married here.

MARGARET: That is an added joy for us.

JOAN: I like your chapel. It is so peaceful, and the light there makes me think of — of the forgiveness of sins.

MARGARET: *(with a start)* What made you say that?

JOAN: I don't know. It came to me this morning at Mass. I thought then that if I had done wrong, I should want to take my sin there, and if I died, I should want to be buried there.....I mean, if I had died in sorrow; because there I could come home and be comforted.

MARGARET: *(standing up)* Sin! Sorrow! Death! What ails you? These are not words or thoughts for a bride. Put them far from you. There should be nothing but joy in your mind now.

JOAN: What do you think is in my lord's mind?

MARGARET: What does it matter? It's not with him you're marrying.

*(JOAN sharply averts her face)*

JOAN: But why doesn't he marry, Margaret? Wouldn't he marry, if he found someone he loved very much — someone who loved him in return?

MARGARET: *(evasively)* He's too old.

JOAN: Nonsense. Look at the king!

MARGARET: Oh, don't look at the King! Stop talking about the King — and about what you don't understand.

JOAN: Well, what the King can do, other men can try.

MARGARET: Heaven forbid.

JOAN: My lord is *not* too old, he's too sorrowful. Sorrow makes men old before their time. But if joy comes back, then the years drop away and the heart grows young again.

MARGARET: And what do you know about it all, 'Signorina Sixteen,' as Philip calls you?

JOAN: *(hastily)* I imagine, of course. And yet I am quite sure I am right.

MARGARET: I don't know about you're being right, but of course you're quite sure. Youth always is.

JOAN: Oh, you are severe!

MARGARET: I'm village born, my lady Joan, but I've lived here so long that I feel I belong now. In every sense of the word, this is home to me; and I've learned to think and talk like the rest of them. But there's one thing I got from my peasant mother that I'll keep to my dying day; a lifetime of mixing with the nobility wouldn't rob me of it.

JOAN: What is it Margaret?

MARGARET: Sense.

JOAN: H'm. Do you know, Margaret, I think your mother must have been an unusual woman?

MARGARET: *(dryly)* She was unusually beautiful.

JOAN: I wasn't thinking of that; I mean, she must have had an unusual character.

MARGARET: Why?

JOAN: To produce two children like you and Bertram. You are like twin pillars of the house, aren't you? If anything happened to either of you, I believe the place would crumble. But it is a pity that Bertram is so lame. How did it happen, Margaret?

MARGARET: Oh — er — it was an accident —

JOAN: But wasn't it due to a fight? He seems to have spent half his life fighting.

MARGARET: Well, it was after a fight, of course.....

JOAN: Oh, I see. I suppose it was after one of those Border raids he talks so much about.

*(MARGARET gives no reply and JOAN does not wait for one.)*

That was a hard fate indeed. He loves horses and fighting and everything active, doesn't he?

*(BERTRAM enters slowly, and approaches. He limps badly*

*and walks with a stick. He, too, has aged considerably.)*
MARGARET: He did.
JOAN: Poor Bertram. I admire him, Margaret. It is he who holds this house together. My lord is such a recluse that without Bertram —
BERTRAM: My lady —
JOAN: Bertram, you shouldn't interrupt when I'm making speeches about you — all complimentary.
BERTRAM: *(Gravely)* My lady is too kind.
JOAN: Well.......and now I've forgotten what I was going to say..... except that you remind me of a bloodhound.
*(MARGARET laughs)*
JOAN: Oh.....I've said the wrong thing. At least, it sounded wrong, though all I meant was "faithful to death".
BERTRAM: *(still grave)* Thank you, my lady. I have some news.
JOAN: I do wish you wouldn't be so formal, Bertram.
BERTRAM: One day, you will be the mistress of this house.
JOAN: Don't start enclosing me in these forbidding stone walls yet! Don't talk as if you couldn't separate me from this ageing fabric I see round me! I'm young, I'm —
MARGARET: Beautiful and a bride. Bertram, have a little sense, even if you haven't any imagination. The girl's sixteen, and getting married.
BERTRAM: My lord, the young master, is coming here to-night.
JOAN: *(starting to her feet)* Philip! To-night? He told me not for four or five days at least.
BERTRAM: *(still with imperturbable gravity)* Events are moving in the North. He will have to go from here almost at once. His messenger has just arrived, worn out with riding. My lady, he wishes to wed with you tomorrow, as soon as may be, for the time is short.
JOAN: But preparations are not complete! It was to have been in a week's time, and there is still much to do. How *can* it be tomorrow?
BERTRAM: My lord expressly says — tomorrow. He will not get here till long past midnight and he begs you will not wait up for him. He will have to leave you soon after the ceremony, which must therefore take place early.
JOAN: Early tomorrow. Then I must see my Lord of Ware —

I must, I must!

BERTRAM: Brother Clement is with him now.

JOAN: *(facing up to them)* Why is Brother Clement always about here with his mysterious little bottles and phials? *(There is silence)*

Well, what is it? Why doesn't he stay in the monastery where he belongs? He's a Lay Brother there, isn't he?

BERTRAM: He is also a physician, and an expert one.

JOAN: *(a slight catch in her breath)* And who is sick? *(Again they do not answer. She stamps her foot at them)* Tell me! Tell me, I say! You talk enough about my being the future mistress of this house, yet you refuse to answer a plain question. Now then, don't keep me waiting any longer! Is my lord — ill?

MARGARET: At times — he is. It is a kind of — fever; a recurrent fever. It can strike him down quite suddenly, and then.....and then —

JOAN: Yes? Go on.

*(BERTRAM and MARGARET exchange glances)*

MARGARET: And then, he imagines things. He often imagines he is back in the past, for instance. Then he has to be kept very quiet and Brother Clement gives him soothing drugs, and looks after him.

JOAN: *(slowly)* I see. Has he always been like this?

BERTRAM: No. Only since he came back from Italy, nearly ten years ago now. He brought home the Lady Nicola, his bride. As you know, she did not live long.

JOAN: I know.

MARGARET: And when she died, the light seemed to go out of my lord's life. He haunts the Chapel, and the tomb where she lies buried.

BERTRAM: I beg your ladyship will not ask us further questions.

JOAN: I won't ask *you*, Bertram, so set your mind at rest. But Margaret's wise, she'll tell me all I want to know, when we're alone. Meanwhile, I must talk to him — *now*.

*(She hurries out R.)*

BERTRAM: You're a woman. Fill in the blanks.

MARGARET: Well —

BERTRAM: But not entirely from your own imagination.

MARGARET: I suppose you want me to tell you the girl's

character inside out. Prophesy her married life with Philip for the next twenty years. Give you the number of children, and all their names. Also, I suppose you'd like the date of my lord's death and the young people's succession to the inheritance.

BERTRAM: This is no matter for joking, Margaret.

MARGARET: It is not. Bertram, are your powers of observation sufficiently acute to detect in our young bride an overpowering interest in my Lord of Ware?

BERTRAM: What are you saying? What are you implying?

MARGARET: I can't understand it. She's gone flying to him now. Philip used to be irresistible to every woman he met. And now, when he's going to be married at last, and everything is hanging on it; and married tomorrow, too —

BERTRAM: Yes?

MARGARET: Apparently he's no longer irresistible, that's all.

BERTRAM: I don't understand your meaning, Margaret. You've got into a habit of brooding and magnifying trifles. It's the solitary life —

MARGARET: I don't brood because I daren't. A husband and son leave too deep an emptiness — so I've been a very busy woman, Bertram, and filled every day with work till I was tired enough to sleep. And now, the most important thing left in my life is this house. We have that much in common. The only difference is that you never had anything else. I had — once.

BERTRAM: But I can't believe there's anything in your suspicions. Surely it's just the girl's natural admiration for an older man? Besides, he's already something of a legend in the North country, and any sort of mystery excites the young.

MARGARET: *(Putting her needlework away methodically)* Well, we must hurry on the preparations, if your messenger is right. I want to decorate the Chapel for tomorrow's service — I want to do it as beautifully as I can.....Nicola lies there.....

BERTRAM: *(Turning away)* A curse on these foreign women! At least this girl is honest English stock. She'll not prove faithless.

MARGARET: It's too late to dream foolish dreams now. She *must* marry Philip tomorrow; but in his place, I'd take her away at once.

BERTRAM: How can he? He is obliged to leave her here with us. He's going.....on a campaign.....Yes! *(His eyes light up. Like an old war horse, he can sniff the battle afar)* You see, we've got to fight. The King has forced it on us. That coming to terms with the Duke of Norfolk was an arranged affair, just to give Henry time to get an army, and this new artillery he's so proud of.

MARGARET: But I thought it was going to be settled *without* a rebellion?

BERTRAM: *(nearly jumping at her to stifle the dreadful word)* Don't use that word, woman! How can you be so foolish — so dangerous. Of course we are not rebels!

MARGARET: Then what are you?

BERTRAM: Loyal folk — loyal to the Church and to the Old Faith, and the old religious houses that have stood England in good stead these many hundred years. It is King Henry who is showing himself a traitor and a monster; despoiling the monasteries and churches; sending one wife to the block that he may wed with another — his sins cry to heaven! An evil spirit possesses him; he usurps the power of the Pope and almost of God himself. There lies his doom. God will not permit it. God will not pardon him.

MARGARET: So, there are storms coming up on the horizon, as usual. Will this house weather them, do you think?

BERTRAM: *(with clenched teeth)* I don't know! This inactivity makes me sick. I wasn't born to keep the books and harry the servants. I want the feel of a horse again, and the bite of steel on steel. I want a camp under the stars, and men I know and trust, who have been with me in old battles — *(He breaks off )* I'm sorry, I must get back to work.
*(He limps away through the exit at the back. MARGARET is just preparing to go, taking her needlework with her, when JOAN enters from R. looking disappointed.)*

JOAN: I can't find him anywhere. What an elusive person he is! He's never where you expect him to be.

MARGARET: I would advise you, my lady, to see that everything is ready for tomorrow. This news has caught us unprepared. There is much to do.

JOAN: Yes, — yes, of course.

MARGARET: I would suggest that you start at once, and do all
you can, and then retire early. You must look fresh and lovely
tomorrow. Come, my lady.

JOAN: In a minute, Margaret.

*(MARGARET goes out, a little uneasily. JOAN tries to tidy
her sewing, but drops it for a book. She glances at the book
then through the window, evidently pre-occupied. WARE
comes in quietly, unperceived by her. He stands behind her,
looking at her intently, and then moves up closer.)*

WARE: I wish I *were* in your dreams, Joan.

*(She turns in surprise, then speaks with sudden intensity.)*

JOAN: You are.

WARE: Thank you. That was more than I dared hope for.

JOAN: Why?

WARE: It is great generosity on your part, my dear. That youth,
beauty, joy and a wedding eve in spring — that all these
things should find any room for me, amazes me. But then,
a crow will sometimes perch for a moment in an April orchard.

JOAN: You — you have always been in my dreams.

WARE: But you have only been here a week! And soon, if
all goes well, you will leave us again. Philip has never looked
on this as his home, you know. And if in the intervals of a
long and happy life, you think of me a little, then I shall
be satisfied.

JOAN: But I thought of you long before I came here!

WARE: How could you? You did not know me.

JOAN: Isn't it possible to think of someone you've never actually
met in the flesh? I've always heard so much about you; somehow I associated you with    with poems and ballards that
I used to read. You fitted into those strange stories and
legends —

WARE: And now you see how foolish it was!

JOAN: But don't you ever dream of people who aren't living
here?

*(He starts and looks at her strangely)*

The past and the future are full of people, aren't they? The
people still unborn, and the people who are — dead.

*(He turns away abruptly. Then bent on changing the subject
picks up one of the books on the window seat.)*

WARE: The people still alive should be quite enough for you!

What were you reading? Poetry, I see.

JOAN: Yes. Look — this is the one I like best.

WARE: "Weeping Cross". That's a sad title.

JOAN: It has another. "Once did I love, and yet I live....."

WARE: *(Laughing)* Well! That's an unusual poem for a bride to read on her wedding eve! "Once did I love, and yet I live". After all, Philip isn't going to murder you, he's only going to marry you.

*(JOAN turns her head away.)*

H'm. Let me read this strange love poem.

*(He reads)*

"Once did I love, and yet I live,
Though love and truth be now forgotten —".

Joan!

JOAN: Oh, read it all. It's a good poem. *(He reads it to himself)* I like the last verse best. *(Repeats softly to herself)*

"Let him not vaunt that gains by loss,
For when that he and time hath proved her,
She may bring him to weeping cross;
I say no more, because I loved her."

*(WARE throws the book down on the seat)*

WARE: Away with it. What made you show me that?

JOAN: You do not care for it?

WARE: Such thoughts and dreams are not for you to-night.

JOAN: And what are for *you*?

WARE: *(with a start)* For me?

JOAN: Yes. What is in your mind, I wonder?

WARE: Joan, never try to wander into my thoughts and dreams. It isn't safe.

JOAN: Why not?

WARE: Because you could find horror and terror, and death; and all the dark things that I pray heaven will never let their shadows fall on your path. You're young. You're still unhurt; and I want you to be very happy. *(Takes her hands.)*

JOAN: I'm always happy — with you.

WARE: *Dropping her hands abruptly)* Don't say those things to me. Keep them for Philip.

JOAN: *(impatiently)* Oh, Philip has been hopelessly spoiled! Dozens of women have been in love with him, and he with them. *(As WARE is about to speak)* Don't deny it. I know they have. He's like a spoiled child who has been fed too many honey cakes.

WARE: Joan! How can you say that!

JOAN: Because I don't believe in living with my eyes shut, and my ears stopped. But you — you're so different. I like being with you.

WARE: Be quiet!

JOAN: I won't! You're so unhappy, it hurts my heart. Philip is unhappy at times, but it only makes him bitter, and cruel. Oh, yes, Philip can be cruel.... but you.... there's no cruelty in you.... just a dark sorrow....

WARE: In which you have no part. If sorrow is my inheritance, then let it die with me. I want you and Philip to begin a new age.

JOAN: In some ways Philip is trying to do that. He hates the despoiling of the monasteries, the forcing of changes on the common people who do not want them; the loss of old valued liberties. It's strange that he could care so much. He's cynical about most things.

WARE: Injustice always roused him to fury.

JOAN: And *you* aren't joining in this rebel army? Though if I call them rebels, Philip snaps at me and says *they* are the loyal folk. He says women always make a habit of calling things by their wrong names.

WARE: *(smiling)* I'm afraid, as usual, the King will favour the women. Whatever they may like to call *themselves*, Henry will only have one name for them — rebels.

JOAN: But don't you see — don't you understand — the penalty for rebellion is — death. *(As he does not answer)* Isn't it?

WARE: Yes.

JOAN: Well, all these thousands of men, all these leaders, young and old, from the finest families there are — what will become of them — if they lose?

WARE: They will be put to death, of course.

JOAN: *(Stamping)* How can you take it so calmly! How can you contemplate the massacre of thousands unmoved! How can you? Or are you certain that they're going to win?

WARE: No. They won't win.

JOAN: Why not? They're right. The King's wrong.

WARE: But the King has the guns.

JOAN: *(turning away)* Your attitude to the whole thing disgusts me. *(Stares through the window)*

WARE: *(coming up behind her)* Joan —

JOAN: Oh, go away. You talk to me about joy and brightness, and keeping all the shadows to yourself, and then you calmly, heartlessly contemplate the death of thousands of innocent men, including Philip. It's abominable.

WARE: Oh, Philip will be safe enough. Never worry about him! I don't. He's always had the devil's own luck.

JOAN: *(turning)* The devil's own luck will hardly keep him safe in a religious uprising, whose every banner is a holy picture, and every countersign a word of Christ's.

WARE: *(smiling again)* Very well. I bow to your superior judgement. But speaking practically, if Henry wins, and decides to play the victorious King, I don't think he'll indulge in a mass murder of the leaders; especially the young nobility. They're rather too valuable. As usual, Philip's youth, charm and birth will save him, but they'll hang the commoners right and left and I expect the elderly ones will be made an example of……. There's old Darcy. He's seventy. I've no doubt at all there's a high gallows waiting for him, on Tower Hill.

JOAN: Aren't you — rather callous — about human life?

WARE: *(narrowing his eyes at her)* No.

JOAN: Don't you care at all?

WARE: For what?

JOAN: Human suffering. Pain, sickness, wounds, death….. *(She can hardly get the word out)* ….. executions…….

WARE: Have you ever seen anyone you loved, die, Joan?

JOAN: *(a little frightened)* I haven't seen anyone die at all.

WARE: No? You haven't seen anyone wounded, struggling, agonised….. *(His voice trails off)*

JOAN: I tamed a white pigeon once….. it got hurt….. somehow. Then one day I found the dogs worrying it to bits in the garden. But it was still beating its wings….. they were covered with blood *(She shivers)* It was horrible. You see, I had loved it, and it trusted me.

WARE: I see. Yes, of course, you loved — the pigeon. *(Suddenly tense)* Don't talk to me like this again. Let me be callous. I can't be sane otherwise…..

JOAN: What do you mean?

WARE: I know too much. I've seen too much — including battle
fields the day after the battle, and all the justifiable executions
that followed. They're always *justifiable*, you see, even the
tortures. The King, the Court, the Parliament, — all the leaders
everywhere — they can always justify everything. And if you
appealed to your dogs in their own language, they'd find
ample justification for what they did to your pigeon.

JOAN: *(sinking on to window seat)* I don't understand it all —

WARE: Who does? But there are moments of beauty, even of
joy. Take them, cherish them, remember them, make them
safe! You will be blessed and happy if you do. Many people
live all their lives even without the moments.

JOAN: *(softly)* You don't. You have had them once. I know,
by the way you speak. Why don't you think of them oftner
and put them against the dark hours?

WARE: The dark *years*! Yes, they are apt to swamp the rest.
But you are so young. You can begin tomorrow — begin
now.

JOAN: I'd like to begin — now. *(She puts a hand out gently
and touches his sleeve)* Don't you understand? I don't want
to marry Philip.

WARE: *(starting back)* But you must — you must! You can't
break with him now. Everything's signed and settled. You
senseless girl! He's coming here tonight.

JOAN: There is still time.

WARE: There is not! And as soon as he leaves you, Philip will
ride straight to danger. You were very solicitous about him
a few months ago.

JOAN: Well, I don't want to see him hanged! I was very fond of
Philip. I'm still fond of him. But I don't love him and I won't
marry him.

WARE: Indeed you will! His heart is set on it and Philip must
marry. Suppose he did come to death, and childless, what
would become of us all? There's too much involved for you
to play fast and loose with your girl's fancies now.

JOAN: *(bitterly)* And you talked of happiness!

WARE: Most women would consider it the same thing as marrying Philip.

JOAN: Then I must be the exception.

WARE: You must be exceptionally foolish. Anyhow, you don't know your own mind.

JOAN: But I do. You see, I did love him once. Strange, isn't it, that I can say that now, when only so short a time ago I loved him still! But it's all in the past. I'd never met anyone like him — charming, clever, handsome — oh, yes, he's all that. But I've stopped loving him.

WARE: Then you'd better find the way to start again, because you are going to marry him tomorrow. Yes, you are. The destiny of this house demands it. There is no escape now.

JOAN: *(wildly)* Yes, there is. There might be! It isn't too late. Don't you see what we might do?

WARE: No, I don't.

JOAN: *(summoning all her courage)* You are the senior. It should be you to make the house safe — you —

WARE: I don't understand.

JOAN: Oh, why do you make me put it so bluntly? Why do you spend your life creeping about in the shadows? Why don't you come out into the sunlight and *live*? I'll help you. I'll never leave you. Philip will soon console himself.
*(Full realization dawns on the Earl. He steps up into the window embrasure and seems to tower above her, for the look on his face has made her cower down on the seat.)*

WARE: *(in a steely voice)* You are going to marry Philip. That is quite settled. As for me, put me out of your thoughts for ever. I can't come out into the light and live — again.

JOAN: *(half whispering)* Why not?

WARE: If you will drag the truth from me, because I am already dead and burried in the Chapel where you and he will stand tomorrow.


CURTAIN

## ACT 1

### SCENE II

*The setting is the same. About 6 weeks have elapsed since Scene 1. It's early evening.*

BERTRAM *is looking through the window, and he is serious, not to say apprehensive.*

HUGH, *the serving man, enters.* BERTRAM *is never so much withdrawn that he is unconscious of what goes on round him. He turns sharply.*

BERTRAM: What is it?

HUGH: Things are looking ugly, sir. As you know the Abbot gave a cold welcome to the King's Commissioners. Now they say he has locked all doors against the King's troops. They are mustering outside the monastery.

BERTRAM: Then it seems that the Abbot is asking for certain death.

HUGH: Yes, sir.

BERTRAM: And perhaps destruction.

HUGH: I'm afraid so, sir. If they hanged the Abbot of Fountains, I don't see why they should spare ours.

BERTRAM: Nor do I. But he isn't "ours" any longer, Hugh.

Times have changed.

HUGH: Changed! They're going from bad to worse as fast as they can with the King to lead them!

BERTRAM: Sh! Be careful, man!

HUGH: And the Abbot will always be "our" Abbot until —

BERTRAM: Until he's hanged?

HUGH: *(miserably)* Oh, sir? I don't understand what's happening. I don't understand these times we live in at all.

BERTRAM: If it's any consolation to you, I don't either.

HUGH: But the whole world — the world we know — is falling to pieces. There always have been Abbeys and shrines and monks.....

BERTRAM: Yes, go on. And Abbots and friars, and hospitality for the wayfarer, care for the sick, and lessons for the poor.

HUGH: Exactly. And now — what are we to think? What are we to believe?

BERTRAM: The King has told us all what to think and what to believe, hasn't he? He's also told us what to expect if we don't

HUGH: But sir, I *can't*. How can I disobey my lord Abbot? On the other hand, how can I disobey my lord the King?

BERTRAM: My poor fellow, I've told you before I don't know the answer to the riddle! It's beyond *me*. I'm not one of your readers or thinkers, Hugh. I've never set much store by my own head-piece. A good strong right arm has been more in my line.

HUGH: Mine, too, sir. You see, I can't even read or write, but I was brought up to obey the Holy Church, and I always tried to do that, because if I don't, I shall go to hell. Now, the King says, if you don't obey *me* above the Church, you'll be imprisoned, or worse and most likely put to death in the end. So it's either hell on earth, or hell to come, it seems to me.

BERTRAM: Well, which do you think you'd prefer?

HUGH: I don't know! I don't want to die, but if I must, I do want to go to heaven. The Priests say the next life lasts a lot longer than this, so what is a poor man to do between them all? Oh, sir, couldn't you decide for me? I'm no scholar and *you* can read and write.

BERTRAM: I don't think reading and writing will settle the question.

HUGH: I don't know. Most questions do seem to be settled

that way in the end. At least, it seems so to us poor ignorant folk. So I'll do what you and my lord do. That will be the simplest way, for I can't think it out for myself.

BERTRAM: My lord is a recluse, as you know. He lives with his books and refuses to take any active part in these happenings.

HUGH: There you are! He's a wise one he is; and that's the result of reading and writing! I wish I had his advantages. So his books tell him to keep out of it, do they? Well, I'll start being a recluse, too, and save my head.

BERTRAM: *(With a start of surprise, stepping nearer the window)* What's that? *(Hugh moves up beside him. BERTRAM points)* Over there – do you see? By my faith – it's the Abbey. Look! (A fierce red glow is suddenly reflected through the window. It falls on the opposite wall and touches the tapestry; it is like the reflection of a red sunset on a winter's day.)

BERTRAM: It can't be – they couldn't do it – no –

HUGH: The Abbey! *(He gives a half-stifled moan and hides his face)*

BERTRAM: The Abbey – the whole monastery – wholesale destruction – but they're mad – mad –

HUGH: *(moaning)* They're devils, devils out of hell! But we shall be punished for this. We shall all go down quick into the pit.

BERTRAM: *(Between his teeth)* How dare they? God, how dare they!

HUGH: When I was sick, they cared for me – over there, and my old father too. They taught my brother his clerkship.

BERTRAM: They taught me all I know. Go quickly and fetch my lord.

*(HUGH hurries out*

*A stealthy figure creeps in from corridor C, muffled in a cloak. It is PHILIP, worn, and bespattered with mud, looking like a hunted fugitive. BERTRAM's quick ears detect him at once, just as a spurt of flame rising higher than the rest suddenly catches him in its reflection.)*

BERTRAM: So you've come.

PHILIP: Yes.

BERTRAM: Any hope left?

PHILIP: None. We're tricked every way, it's just a massacre

now — political massacre, not a battle.

BERTRAM: Then the world *has* gone to the devil.

PHILIP: And with speed. They've hanged Darcy, and Aske, and Hussey.

BERTRAM: And — you?

PHILIP: They're after me now. I've eluded them so far..... I didn't want to bring any more trouble to this house. You must believe that, Bertram. It was my idea to take shelter in the monastery until the danger was past — but you see — *(Gestures to window)*

BERTRAM: They must be mad! How can they, how dare they do it?

PHILIP: I hope the Abbot escapes. If he doesn't, a mock trial and a hanging for him. He isn't the only one. Already they've hanged the Abbot of Whalley and the Abbot of Fountains —

BERTRAM: Yes. We heard.

PHILIP: And what do you think of it all?

BERTRAM: I think God has forsaken us.

PHILIP: *(with a short laugh)* He hadn't far to go..... Well, Bertram, I've only come for one thing, and then I'll relieve you of my dangerous presence. Where is she?

BERTRAM: I will call my lady immediately. *(Moves to door R)*

PHILIP: Six weeks ago to-day.....

BERTRAM: *(formally)* She has grieved for you.

*(LORD WARE enters, followed by HUGH)*

WARE: You!

PHILIP: It's only that I want to see Joan — I must see her just for a few minutes before I go. It'll probably be good-bye. I'm on the run, and I won't get you all under suspicion.

WARE: *(to HUGH)* Call my lady here at once.

*(HUGH goes out)*

WARE: Of course you must stay here.

PHILIP: No, — my idea was the monastery, but — *(he looks towards the window and shrugs)* I think the whole world's on fire, uncle.

WARE: I think it is.

BERTRAM: Since the monastery can no longer shelter you —

PHILIP: Ah! They had many good hiding places there!

BERTRAM: And there is still one — The best of them all, left here. Only we three know the secret. Surely that would be the best thing, my lord? *(He goes to panelling, right)* It's a fair sized room, too.

PHILIP: *(following)* No, I'm not going to be your skeleton in the cupboard. But I'm afraid I must claim its hospitality for to-night, at least. The soldiers are too close to be healthy, and they'll probably come here on some pretext or other, though I swear none of them saw me. They were too much engrossed with the fire.

WARE: Open it, Bertram.

*(Together, they pull back the secret-panel, and disclose the entrance to the hiding place, large enough for a man to squeeze through.)*

PHILIP: The state bedroom. A little musty, I think. *(Puts his head in and sniffs.)*

WARE: But you must admit you have had some notable predecessors!

PHILIP: Yes....... And I seem to remember that they mostly came to notable ends. *(Turns)* Let me get my fill of fresh air first.

*(Moves to window. They notice for the first time that he walks with a bad limp. He stumbles and almost collapses on to the window-seat.)*

WARE: *(Striding after him)* Why in heaven's name didn't you tell us you were hurt.

BERTRAM: My lord —

PHILIP: It's nothing. My horse fell — fell on me, No, what am I saying? *(Puts his hands to his head)* What did happen? The horse stumbled — we fell — he rolled — on my leg. He, I — I did the rest of the way on foot. I'm tired you see; that's what it is, I'm tired. *(He subsides)*

WARE: Get some wine — and food — quickly.

*(BERTRAM hurries out)*

Steady Philip. Your luck holds. It always has — it always will.

PHILIP: No, no. Not now. There's a change somewhere. I feel that something has broken it at last, though I don't know what it is.

*(JOAN appears in the entrance and hurries forward)*

JOAN: Philip!

WARE: Careful! He's hurt badly. His horse fell, and rolled.

JOAN: *(kneeling beside him)* Oh, Philip!

WARE: He struggled here on foot. He's a fugitive, Joan. Do you understand? We must hide him tonight, the soldiers are too close for safety. As soon as they disperse, he must get to the coast.

JOAN: And go abroad, I see.

WARE: Yes, but you'll follow him, of course. They can't have anything against you.

*(BERTRAM returns with food and wine, some of which they more or less pour down PHILIP's throat. He stirs.)*

JOAN: Oh why, why did he come? Why didn't he escape to the coast straight away, without coming here?

PHILIP: *(opening his eyes)* Because I'm a bad sailor, my dear. I couldn't face the thought of coming-to on board ship, without even the memory of you to sustain me. *(Takes her hands, as she does not answer)* I came to see you, of course. Aren't you glad?

JOAN: *(nervously)* Yes, — oh, yes. Thank you Philip.

WARE: You must stay here till all danger's past. *(To JOAN)* mustn't he?

JOAN: *(lifelessly)* Yes, he must.

*(HUGH hurries in. Sounds of hammering on doors and shouting offstage.)*

HUGH: *(scared)* May it please you, my Lord, they're at the gate, a dozen of them at least! It was "Open, in the King's name" They wish to see — that is, they know.....

*(Glances miserably at PHILIP)*

PHILIP: *(struggling to his feet)* Someone did see me, after all, is that it?

HUGH: Yes, sir. They know you're here, one of them tracked you and went back to fetch the others. He guessed you were a fugitive from your walk. They want the man with a limp.

WARE: Tell them I will come at once. *You've* seen no fugitive, understand?

*(Exit HUGH)*

WARE: Now, the hiding place.

PHILIP: *(taking JOAN's hands)* Good-bye, my dear. I could have made you very happy — if I'd had the chance.

JOAN: Good-bye.

PHILIP: Try to forgive us all the trouble and the bloodshed.

Only remember — that I loved you.....
*(They assist him through the door. BERTRAM thoughtfully pushes the food and wine in after him, and they close the panel. JOAN has been looking at it like one transfixed, and when the click of its closing comes, she falls abruptly to the floor. The two men hurry to her side.)*

BERTRAM: They mustn't find her like this. They'd be suspicious at once. It would be best to carry her away, my lord. I'll go down to talk to them till you come, and give them some wine. That'll help drown their impatience..... ......for they grow impatient.

*(He has caught sight of HUGH who has diffidently returned to say that the King's men will not be kept waiting.)*

I suppose that's why you've come back, Hugh?

HUGH: Yes, sir. Their manners are offensive, sir.

WARE: No one could have sworn it was he, creeping through the twilight.

BERTRAM: There's bound to be a doubt. I'll play on that. *(As WARE raises JOAN)* Why not carry her to the Chapel, my lord? That's furthest away. They'll think the pious lady has fainted at her prayers. Light no candles.

WARE: She'll be afraid.

BERTRAM: Then stay by her side a few moments to comfort her, in case her senses return too quickly. I'll deal with the men. You can trust me.

WARE: That I can, Bertram. *(He lifts up JOAN and carries her out by door R.)*

BERTRAM: Now, Hugh — quickly. Did anyone recognise the young master as he came in?

HUGH: I don't think so, sir. He had his own key to the postern gate and twilight was falling

BERTRAM: Good. These men — did any one of them actually see his *face*?

HUGH: No, sir. Only one man followed him and gussed him to be a fugitive. They are asking for the man with a limp.

BERTRAM: I see. So only *you* really know of the young master's arrival?

HUGH: Yes, sir.

BERTRAM: And I can count on you to forget it, with all speed?

HUGH: Yes, sir.

BERTRAM: Now, while I go and put them off the scent, I want you to take a message to my lord. *(He unhooks a small bunch of keys from his belt)* Give him these. He'll understand; and say —

HUGH: Yes, sir?

BERTRAM: Just say, I wish him good-night.

*(HUGH goes out.)*

*(BERTRAM nerves himself for the moment, and grasps his stick.)*

They want the man with the limp —

*(As he moves across to the corridor exit, he passes PHILIP's hiding place. He falters a moment; then with an air of determination, he goes out.*

*Off-stage shouts increase, with cries of "There he is — the man with the limp — after him — after him! Bring your rope........")*


CURTAIN

## "AND YET I LIVE"

### ACT II

*The setting is the same. A few weeks have elapsed.*
JOAN *is sitting in the window embrasure, doing needlework.*

PHILIP *opposite, is regarding her intently.*
JOAN *evidently feels ill at ease under his gaze. Suddenly she pricks her finger, and with an exclamation of annoyance, stops work, and sucks the pricked place.*

PHILIP: Do you like needlework, Joan?
JOAN: No, I hate it. *(resumes work)*
PHILIP: Why do you do it then?
JOAN: One must do something — if one's a woman.
PHILIP: You could talk to me.
JOAN: I can do both things, can't I?
PHILIP: *(after a slight pause)* Joan, when did you discover you weren't in love with me any more?
   *(JOAN stops her work abruptly and looks away confused)*
JOAN: What do you mean? I never said —
PHILIP: Spare me the protests, please. I'm not a fool. And hitherto I've always considered you intelligent — for a girl.
JOAN: But I never said —
PHILIP: Not in the actual words. That was hardly necessary when

everything about you shouted the truth at me. Ever since I came back you've been crying out to me — wordlessly — "I don't love you — I don't love you — go away —"

JOAN: *(distressed)* Oh, Philip.

PHILIP: Go on. Finish it..... "I didn't mean to hurt you, I'm so sorry, Philip." Well?

JOAN: *(coldly)* You seem to have forestalled me?

PHILIP: I'm right. You can't deny it.

JOAN: *(almost in a whisper)* I don't.

PHILIP: Then how did it start? And when did you find you no longer loved me?

JOAN: *(with bent head)* When I came here.

PHILIP: Oh. And what happened here?

*(JOAN averts her head and does not answer)*

PHILIP: Answer me. What happened here?

JOAN: I — I don't know. Something — changed. I just didn't feel the same about you, though I loved you once. That's all.

PHILIP: *Is* it?

JOAN: Yes.

PHILIP: I wonder if you're telling me the truth?

JOAN: Have you ever known me lie to you?

PHILIP: I'm not sure yet.

JOAN: Please don't let's quarrel your last evening. You'll leave to-night, and then you'll go far away, almost alone.

PHILIP: That won't worry you.

JOAN: And who knows how long it will be before we meet again?

PHILIP: Who indeed?

JOAN: Philip, what are you going to do when you get to France?

PHILIP: Oh, travel to the South, by easy stages. I've a little land there, left me by my mother. It's — it's rather beautiful, you know, in Provence. I used to think that perhaps you would like to come. But now, I see that you would hate it. And I couldn't bear to have you there, in the middle of all that beauty — hating it.

JOAN: I'd never been away from our house in the whole of my life, till I came here. How could I tell now whether I should like France, or not?

PHILIP: Easily, if you loved me.

*(MARGARET enters)*

JOAN: Yes, Margaret?

MARGARET: My lord is not well. I think it's a return of one of his old fevers. I've sent Clement to him.

JOAN: And what does Clement say?

MARGARET: That he needs sleep. He has gone to prepare a soothing drug. My poor unhappy lord! Ever since — since he lost Bertram, he's been unable to rest.

JOAN: I know.

MARGARET: He was in the library, poring over his books, as usual, but Clement has made him go to his room and lie down. He — he asked for you, my lady, *(With a glance at PHILIP)* He wishes to speak with you both, before you leave, sir…. But there's no hurry for the moment if you are — if you are busy here.

JOAN: We'll go in a few minutes. That will do, Margaret.

MARGARET: Thank you, my lady. *(She goes out.)*

PHILIP: He's interfering with the best intentions, of course.

JOAN: Yes.

PHILIP: And they'll probably be quite useless…. does Margaret give you the feeling of — of —

JOAN: *(Covering her face with her hands and almost crying)* I can't bear to think of it — Bertram, of all people! And he was all she had left….

PHILIP: Oh! So that's the grudge against me?

JOAN: *(Pulling herself up)* What do you mean?

PHILIP: Are you implying I could have helped that wretched business? Don't you see it's eaten like poison into my soul?

JOAN: He shouldn't have done it.

PHILIP: Agreed. And how often since then I've wished to God he'd let me hang in peace! You would all have been your usual happy selves by this time.

JOAN: Don't sneer, Philip.

PHILIP: I'm not. The result of Bertram's nobility is that my uncle is more morose than ever — he's seen out of his library less and less, and now he's ill. You are more — er — distant than before; Margaret is breaking her heart in silence, and I have become audibly objectionable, apparently.

JOAN: I hate you when you talk like this!

PHILIP: Only then?

JOAN: Oh, Philip, please don't let's quarrel! We're doing it again. It isn't worth it.

PHILIP: Agreed. But do you seriously think for one moment I should have let Bertram do that, if I'd known? I couldn't hear or see anything in that hiding place. And by the time they let me out he was — he was — it was all over.

JOAN: Yes, yes. I know you couldn't help it. Of course I know.

PHILIP: Well then, what's the grievance;

JOAN: I haven't one. It's just that — oh, I haven't got over it yet. It was so horrible. It was his lameness that made it all the worse — don't you see? You should.

PHILIP: Oh, so you've found out about that, have you?

JOAN: About what?

PHILIP: About why he was lame?

JOAN: Wasn't he wounded in a Border fight?

PHILIP: No, he wasn't.

JOAN: What *did* happen then?

PHILIP: You may as well know, as I seem to have very little left to lose in your eyes. I did it.

JOAN: You! I don't understand. How did you do it?

PHILIP: I fought him... *(points)* down that long corridor — at night — I forced him against a window — he crashed through. They thought he was dead. So did I.

JOAN: *(recoiling in horror)* You — you of all people! How could you?

PHILIP: We quarrelled. I had provocation, I assure you.

JOAN: But Bertram! So good, so kind, so utterly faithful, and devoted to the house.

PHILIP: Yes. All the virtues — hadn't he?

JOAN: What could *he* have done to provoke you?

PHILIP: Well, there I think we'd better stop, for the sake of all concerned.

JOAN: And who was concerned?

PHILIP: Others — beside the two of us.

JOAN: *(after a fraction of hesitation)* — My lord?

PHILIP: Well yes, in a way. But that's the end. I've confessed enough for one day, haven't I? Added to which, I hate confession at the best of times.

JOAN: Why did you confess then — and just to me?

PHILIP: *(turning in real distress)* Oh, Joan, Joan! Do you under-

stand so little, after all? *Only* to you! Don't you see, I love
you in spite of everything.... Confession is only bearable —
possible even — where love is. It was one of my better
moments. I know they're rare. But I thought you'd understand.

JOAN: I'm sorry —

PHILIP: Oh, for God's sake stop being sorry for me! If you can't
love me, leave it at that.
*(Strides away from her. JOAN almost involuntarily puts her
hand into her bag of silks, then starts back, as though something had burnt her.)*

JOAN: Philip.

PHILIP: *(without turning)* Yes?

JOAN: There's something I want to ask you. It's about — Nicola.
*(PHILIP spins round, as if he had been caught unawares)*

PHILIP: What do you mean? Nicola — Nicola is... only a legend.
You don't know anything about her... do you?

JOAN: I want to know more.

PHILIP: *(sharply)* Well, you can't.

JOAN: But I want to, I must. Don't you understand, she's
brooding about this house still? Only "brooding" sounds like
a dark forbidding presence, and she was never that, was she?

PHILIP: No.

JOAN: Surely she was young and bright — yes, I always think
of a light, when I think of her.

PHILIP: Why?

JOAN: She had yellow hair, hadn't she? It must have looked
like an aureole when the sun caught it.

PHILIP: Stop stop.

JOAN: Why will none of you talk to me about Nicola?

PHILIP: Since we won't, why do you persist in trying to make
us?

JOAN: Because I want to know, and I've a right to know, now
that I belong to this house and this family.

PHILIP: Let the past alone. Let the dead bury it's dead. Nicola
is dead.

JOAN: Is she?

PHILIP: *(with a start)* What do you mean — is she? Well, what
do you mean? Are you mad?

JOAN: There are days when I feel Nicola is much more alive

than I am. She is more alive to my lord still, than I can ever
be.

PHILIP: Oh, yes. He isn't quite sane where Nicola is concerned.
You'd better let the subject alone with him.

JOAN: I have to. But I'm not going to let it alone with you.

PHILIP: Joan, there's a certain ruthlessness about you that I've
never met in a woman before. There are moments when I
find it alarming. I suppose it's because you grew up without
any women round you, except servants.

JOAN: No. It's not that. It's something quite different. It's
something that belongs to this house, so you ought to understand. People who live in this house seem to get obsessed
by one idea. I have one idea dominating my whole life. I want
something so much that I'll sacrifice anything and anybody
to get it. And get it I will, and at all costs. If it rests with me,
I'll pay the utmost price.

PHILIP: By heaven, Joan, if your father and your brothers had
your spirit, they wouldn't be fugitives now!

JOAN: Had I been a son, instead of Roger, I should never have
joined this mad enterprise. But they cast me off — they had
arranged my marriage to you, quite heartlessly. I never had
any love from them, and I never gave them any back. If my
mother had lived, things might not have been the same.

PHILIP: It's a pity that some of that unused love couldn't be
given to me. You're different, Joan. Even your ruthlessness
is different, and yet I've seen you cry over a sick puppy!
Rather inconsistent, aren't you?

JOAN: Not more than you. Why did you suddenly return to
England, and throw your lot in with these rebels, when you'd
been living a selfish and lazy life in France for years?

PHILIP: You may not believe it, but I had a gleam of idealism.
I came back and found things rotten through and through,
tyranny rampant, and a new distasteful, destructive order
being thrust on the unhappy people. I hate tyranny and
injustice. I hate to see the common people suffer. Oh, yes,
I do. It makes me feel like you when you watched the puppy.
At least, as far as I remember, you couldn't watch it. You
asked Bertram to put it out of its misery.

JOAN: Yes — I see. We're both inconsistent. I suppose everyone
is. But Philip, I — I've found something. Something belonging

to Nicola.

PHILIP: Nicola again! How did *you* get it?

JOAN: It's strange, but my lord asked me to look over some of her things, in the little west room, where she used to sit and read, and sometimes play and sing. You know he has left it untouched all these years. Dust and decay are everywhere. But one day, he asked me if I would go in there and try to set it in order a little. He could not bear the servants to do it, and not even Margaret had been allowed to enter.

PHILIP: *(incredulously)* He asked *you*? I can hardly believe it!

JOAN: Well, I told him he ought to, of course. He'll never stop brooding and creeping about in the shadows, with a locked room in the house, and a darkness like it in his heart.

PHILIP: I see.

JOAN: *(fumbling in her bag)* I was looking at one of Nicola's books. This fell out. I think it's a piece of her hair tied to parchment with some writing on it.

PHILIP: Give it to me at once!

JOAN: *(backing)* I want to know what it means. Some of it is in your writing — in latin. But I can understand that it's a love poem.

PHILIP: Joan!

JOAN: Underneath there's something in another script, hers I suppose. First, there's a message; then, as far as I can make out, it means "We have been separated like night from day. Henceforward we shall be together in an everlasting twilight."

PHILIP: Joan! *(He grips her hands savagely and tears the packet from her. JOAN gives an exclamation of pain and sinks down on the seat.)*

PHILIP: So you found *that*! God, this place is full of ghosts!

JOAN: And *you* loved Nicola.

PHILIP: Yes I loved her once. Someone else said that, It was you, wasn't it? You loved me — once.

JOAN: *(looking away)* I was right. Nicola is not dead. Her yellow hair is still between us, between you and me, between my lord and the world.

PHILIP: She *is* dead, I tell you! I swear to you she's dead.

JOAN: And I'll swear another thing — she isn't buried in that tomb in the chapel.

*(PHILIP stifles a scream and backs against the window. He drops the packet as if it had been touched by the plague. WARE comes in. He walks uncertainly, staring in front of him. JOAN picks up the packet and puts it in her dress.)*

WARE: Where are you? Where are you? I sent for you and you did not come. I called you and you did not answer. Where are you?

JOAN: I am here. *(She crosses to him quickly.)*

WARE: *(As he puts his arms round her)* You have grown taller, sweet, your head used not to come above my shoulder.

JOAN: My, lord, are you ill.

WARE: Yes, my head burns strangely. Bertram thinks it is a tough of fever. He should know. He's lain wounded through the night more than once. A rare soldier, Bertram. Is he not?

JOAN: Why, certainly, my lord.

WARE: *(caressing her)* Why do you stand in the shadows, sweet?

JOAN: I am not in the shadows, my lord.

WARE: Yes, yes. They are all about your face and hair. I cannot see its gold. My head is so hot, Nicola.
*(JOAN starts away from him.)*
Do not start away from me.

JOAN: You are ill. You must lie down. I will call Clement. Come with me. Come — *(She guides him to the door, half-supporting him. When nearly there, he stops.)*

WARE: I have had bad dreams. I dreamed there was a darkness upon the house, because you were dead...dead...and buried in the Chapel. Kiss me, to prove you are alive, Nicola, and not in the cold tomb.

JOAN: *(Winding her arms about him and kissing him passionately)* I swear I am alive! Nicola is not in the tomb! *(She helps him through the doorway R. PHILIP sinks on the window seat. He shivers and covers his face with his hands.)*

PHILIP: So that's what she wants!
*(He crosses to the entrance — back — and calls)*
Margaret! Margaret!

MARGARET: *(Off)* I come. *(She hurries in)*

PHILIP: Margaret, my lord came here. He has a bad fever... He's very ill, Margaret.

MARGARET: I'm not surprised. He won't eat or sleep —

says he can't. It would wear down the strongest man, and he's not that.

PHILIP: Don't go for a moment, Margaret. Joan is with him — my loving wife.

MARGARET: *(startled at his tone)* What do you mean?

PHILIP: What I say. Joan is my wife, isn't she? She's in love, isn't she? But with whom, Margaret, with whom?

MARGARET: *(Backing away from him, afraid)* With you, of course.

PHILIP: Well lied, Margaret — good, faithful old Margaret. You're another Bertram, aren't you? And as usual, I'm the villain of the piece. No, by Heaven, but I'm not this time! I'm the injured one for a change. What a sweet revenge, if only he knew!

MARGARET: What are you talking about?

PHILIP: Revenge. No, vengeance. It sounds better and more biblical. God enjoys vengeance, and it's just. We misguided humans enjoy revenge, and it's damnable.

MARGARET: Oh, don't talk so —

PHILIP: Listen, Margaret, have you forgiven me for harming Bertram?

MARGARET: Of course. Long ago.

PHILIP: And — well, you know I was powerless to stop him saving my life, or else I swear he should never have done it. You do believe that, Margaret?

MARGARET: Yes, of course I do.

PHILIP: But for all this, for everything I've done, knowingly and unknowingly — do you hate me, Margaret?

MARGARET: No. I don't hate anyone.

PHILIP: Margaret — Margaret — you put me to shame. You and Bertram always did. His ghost will be about me — always.

MARGARET: No, no! He never wanted it to be like that!

PHILIP: I know. But we can never tell the destiny of an action. It is never what we imagine, when we act. We weave our own web of doom, and catch ourselves in it unawares.

MARGARET: I dare not think. I cannot reason now. I have only — faith.

PHILIP: I envy you, Margaret. You have all that matters. Listen Do you know why Bertram and I fought that night I lamed him?

MARGARET: No.

PHILIP: No? What a pair! So you never knew what provoked me to draw on him?

MARGARET: No.

PHILIP: Bertram was right, of course ... well, time has brought its revenge, but it brings no comfort to you, my poor Margaret. I must leave here to-night, as arranged.

MARGARET: Not if my lord is ill! You can't. It would be heartless.

PHILIP: No, Margaret. For once it would not! I'm going to France, as I planned. I hope there's a war on somewhere. But, of course, there always is. It is my intention to join in.

MARGARET: Oh, sir, — not again!

PHILIP: But this is for the last time, I promise you. It is a humble act of expiation. At the moment, I feel humble and expiatory. You look incredulous?

MARGARET: You shouldn't go!

PHILIP: Dear, kind Margaret, believe me this once, for I'm too tired and too unhappy to lie to anyone now, least of all you. It's best for you all that I go, — and to-night. Better still, I never come back.

MARGARET: My lord might ask for you.

PHILIP: If he does, it would be better for both of us if he didn't find me. He's wild in his head. He thinks Joan is — Nicola. *(MARGARET stifles an exlamation)*
Joan — er — lets him think so.

MARGARET: It might be dangerous to cross him.

PHILIP: Once, it would have been dangerous to cross *me.*
*(CLEMENT enters. He was once a Lay Brother at the Monastery, and it is too soon yet for him to be entirely accustomed to secular life. He is a physician by inclination and training, and as such has taken up his residence at Ware, since the breaking up of the Monastery.)*

MARGARET: What news? My lord?

CLEMENT: He is a very sick man. This is a dangerous fever of the brain. He must not be left alone.

MARGARET: *(To PHILIP)* There! You shall not go!

PHILIP: You have ample numbers to watch and care for him, haven't you, Brother — I mean, Clement?

CLEMENT: Yes. We lack no help. He must be kept very quiet and, above all things, he must not be crossed, or worried or contradicted. This fever has been slowly burning for some time and now it has come to full blaze. He is suffering from a delusion.

PHILIP: I know. He thinks my wife is — Nicola.

CLEMENT: It might prove fatal to undeceive him too abruptly. The lady Joan is an excellent nurse and helper. He thinks it is his wife caring for him. I beg you, sir, let him think so at least for a few hours. It may save him. He almost sleeps after my drug, and when he wakes, his brain may clear.

PHILIP: H'm. It isn't very long since you were a Priest, is it, Clement?

CLEMENT: You mistake. I was a Lay Brother.

PHILIP: It would not be wise, would it, to see my lord before I go?

CLEMENT: No, I fear not, sir. I would not have him disturbed while the drug works. I trust this stupor will pass to natural sleep.

PHILIP: I understand.

CLEMENT: There is one more thing, sir. As you probably know, the masons have been working on my Lady Nicola's tomb.

PHILIP: *(Spinning round)* I did *not* know! I've lived a close life up here these last weeks, haven't I?

CLEMENT: I thought my lady, your wife, would have told you. She was directing them.

PHILIP: She!

CLEMENT: Since Bertram died, my lord has been like a man without his right hand. He has hardly stirred from his room, except to go to his library. He has never once been down in to the Chapel. The masons had been carving and decorating the tomb but these last weeks only my lady has seen and directed them.

PHILIP: *(with a dry mouth)* Well?

CLEMENT: The master mason is a godly man, he keeps what piety these dreadful days have left us. He has been troubled in his mind of late, and has spoken to Father John and to me.

PHILIP: Spoken of what?

CLEMENT: He feels it to be some kind of sacrilege to carve words of pious grief, and prayer; to insert the date of my lady's death, and of how all sorrowed for her.

PHILIP: And so they did.

CLEMENT: Yes. But it is against his conscience to do all this on an empty tomb!

PHILIP: Empty! You lie — you are both mad. How can it be empty? My lady died — eight years and more ago, didn't she? Margaret?

MARGARET: *(almost inaudibly)* Yes, — yes.

PHILIP: Well then. Don't come to me with your ghoulish tales. And don't stand there gaping, Margaret, as if you had seen a ghost. Go! And see if you can do anything to relieve my lady. Perhaps now he's drowsy, my wife can stop her play acting... and find time to say good-bye to me. Send her at once. I leave almost immediately.

MARGARET: As you wish. *(She goes out R.)*

*(PHILIP is extremely restless, fidgeting and walking about.)*

PHILIP: *(CLEMENT looks at him fixedly.)* Can't you stop looking at me? Better still, can't you go?

CLEMENT: If ever I have seen a man troubled in his conscience, you are that man.

PHILIP: What has my conscience got to do with you? Get out of your monastic thoughts, as you've got out of its habit! We're in a new age, and a new world, now.

CLEMENT: Will you see Father John?

PHILIP: I will not. Of what do you accuse me?

CLEMENT: Of an unquiet mind and a troubled spirit. These things speak of sin committed. What have you done?

PHILIP: That is nothing to do with you. You are not Lord here.

CLEMENT: Neither are you — yet.

PHILIP: I've no wish for it, believe me! If he died to-night I would never live here. It's a cursed and haunted place. Also, England's not safe for me yet.

CLEMENT: Before you go, what are your orders to the masons? My lord is in no fit state to issue orders. As his heir, what do you wish? Is the decoration of the tomb to go on? Are they to continue with their false inscriptions in praise of the lady who lies — elsewhere?

*(PHILIP stops his pacing abruptly and presses his fist against his head. JOAN has come in unperceived and has heard the*

*last words. She stands in the doorway R.)*

CLEMENT: Well? Your answer?

PHILIP: *(almost chattering)* How do you know whether the tomb is empty or not? I don't know what you mean. I don't know what you're talking about. It's lies and imagination and desecration. Do as you like. Do anything you like. I shall be out of it. I shan't be here. I'm going — now.

*(He wheels round to rush from the hall. The doorway is blocked by* JOAN's *motionless form.)*

JOAN: *(coldly)* I've come to say good-bye, Philip.

*(For the first time in his life,* PHILIP *senses a growing personal defeat.)*

PHILIP: I — I leave at once. I will not disturb my uncle.

JOAN: No. The soothing drug works. He sleeps now, and Margaret is watching by him. But I must return.

PHILIP: *(Sarcastically)* Of course. Well, why don't you?

JOAN: Because there is one thing I want to ask you before you go.

PHILIP: What is that?

JOAN: What did you do with Nicola?

*(PHILIP draws his breath quickly)*

Now don't break into denials. Don't start calling us all mad. You loved Nicola. That's admitted. You'd plotted to go away with her the night she died. Oh, yes, I've made that much out from the parchment. It wasn't difficult. You were to live together in the twilight of remorse and sin — I suppose in Provence.

CLEMENT: That night, Bertram provoked you and you fought. I was here; I remember they called me to the Lady Nicola.

PHILIP: Well, she was dead, wasn't she? You've seen plenty of dying and dead, doing your good works. You can recognise death when you meet it, I suppose — or can't you?

CLEMENT: I thought she was dead. She was in the Chapel. I prayed by her. To my everlasing shame — I slept over my prayers; it was so strong, so confused a sleep, that looking back I wonder if it was natural. I have had more experience of drugs since then. I believe they have always been one of your interests?

*(PHILIP does not answer.)*

JOAN: Yes.

CLEMENT: When my senses cleared, my lady was already nailed into her coffin. You had ridden away in the night. You were always famous for your sudden, swift disappearances in the dark. My lord, distracted with grief, had kept his room, and had never looked on the face of his dead wife since she breathed her last.

PHILIP: What is the use of you relating these old facts now? Where are they leading you? What good will it do you? What can you prove? — nothing!

CLEMENT: I accuse you of stealing my lord your uncle's wife by sickening treachery. She was not dead, and you took her.

PHILIP: You daren't accuse me like this — no-one would believe your story. And you daren't start such a train of thought in my uncle's mind, especially now. He'd never be a sane man again.

JOAN: It's true, isn't it, Philip? You and your uncle get obsessions. It's a family trait, as I said. You were both obsessed by Nicola. That night she — nearly died but not quite. You *did* take her away, Philip!

PHILIP: Oh, stop these mad stories!

JOAN: Philip, I must know! If you've any shred of honour left — is Nicola still alive?

PHILIP: No, she's dead, Joan. Before heaven I swear it. She's been dead these many years. God rest her — for she risked her soul for my sake.

JOAN: And where is she now?

PHILIP: *(With an unsteady laugh)* Heaven or Hell — but according to the teaching of the Church, probably the latter. *(He moves to JOAN.)*

JOAN: Don't kiss me — don't touch me.

PHILIP: You're a hard woman, Joan.

JOAN: And you?

PHILIP: By the inescapable justice of things, I've loved you truly and well, with the best love of my life. And I love you still. And this is the result.

JOAN: *(evenly)* Yes. I'm beginning to hate you.

PHILIP: Don't triumph yet, Joan. I've paid for loving you, haven't I? As much as Nicola paid for loving me, or my lord for his love for her. But I'll tell you one thing. I'm not going to leave you here to act Nicola's part.

CLEMENT: It won't be necessary when he wakes. I've seen him like this before. The delusion will pass, after natural sleep. He's been sleepless and tormented for weeks. And you — will you go unconfessed, unrepentant, unshriven?

PHILIP: I've confessed to nothing, and I never will.

JOAN: *(with force)* You will.

PHILIP: What do you mean? You can't make me.

JOAN: If it's to recover my lord's peace of mind, I can!

PHILIP: You daren't tell him your mad suspicions! You daren't! He'd be crazed himself for life, at the idea of it.

JOAN: He might not.

PHILIP: Anyhow, I shan't be here to see. This is final. I'm going for good. Won't you kiss me good-bye Joan?

JOAN: No. I can't see your face. It's hidden in Nicola's yellow hair.

PHILIP: *(turning to CLEMENT, bitterly)* And would you want me to do penance after *that?*

*(PHILIP picks up his cloak, and throws it savagely over his arm. He moves opposite JOAN and looks intently at her.)*

PHILIP: You're my wife. Why shouldn't you come, after all? It's true, times are dangerous, and we arranged for you to wait. We may both get arrested by the King's men. What does it matter now? A wife should share her husband's hardships. Well, shouldn't she?

JOAN: I will not come.

PHILIP: You will, if I say so. Why should I leave you here — with him? I know what you want, Joan; what you'd sacrifice anybody and anything to get. And that knowledge has made all the difference. I don't care if we never reach the end of the journey, but we're going to start.

JOAN: I will not come.

CLEMENT: You cannot take her against her will.

PHILIP: *My* will rules here, if my lord is sick. Come, Joan. Prepare for a long ride through the night.

JOAN: I will never come. I hate you.

PHILIP: If you don't come of your own free will, I shall have to take you.

JOAN: As you took Nicola. Alone, at dead of night. Through the postern gate you always use. A servant well bribed... So you think history can repeat itself!

*(PHILIP makes to seize her in his arms to carry her out. She whips out a dagger and backs a step till she leans against a pillar.)*

JOAN: I'm not Nicola! And I won't stop at murder! I hate you and I won't come with you. If you take me with you by force, I'll find some way to kill myself and you. I mean it. *(She is tense and determined. Suddenly PHILIP relaxes.)*

PHILIP: I can't face living with your hate, Joan. I'm not a fiend! Don't look at me like that, as if I were your mortal enemy. *(pleading)* Joan!

*(She does not relax)*

PHILIP: Then may your own love turn to death! May the doom of this house, that fell on Nicola and on me, fall on you too! May you die in sorrow! *(He rushes out)*

JOAN: *(As CLEMENT hurries forward to support her)* No! I *will* change the doom of this house! Life and death have struggled here like bitter enemies...but they shall be reconciled. I believe in life........

CURTAIN

## ACT III

*The setting is the same.*

*It is late autumn, 1537. Several months have elapsed since Act II.*

*The old Provencal song, quoted in this act, is by Peire Cardenal (13th century troubadour poet.) The translation used is the one quoted in "A Wayfarer in Provence" by E.I. Robson and J.R.E. Howard.*

CLEMENT *is standing in the window embrasure, holding a phial of liquid up against the light.* JOAN *is pacing up and down, evidently in agitation.*

JOAN: Clement, he's going down to the chapel *now*. He insists. We can't keep the knowledge from him any longer.

CLEMENT: No. *(He turns from his scrutiny almost with a sigh of regret. He still holds the phial lovingly between his fingers.)* I think you were ill-advised to have every trace of the Lady Nicola's tomb taken away.

JOAN: No, Clement! This illusion of his must be shattered. This brooding obsession must be broken, and Nicola's ghost laid for ever — but not here.

CLEMENT: Drastic measures.

JOAN: Drastic *remedies* for desperate cases. He'll have to go by himself, and find the tomb is not there. *I* can't go with him… Oh, Clement, for months I've dreaded this moment, and now it's upon me!

CLEMENT: Yes.

JOAN: He *is* better, isn't he, Clement?

CLEMENT: Wonderfully better. When I think what he was the night Philip left, I marvel at it.

JOAN: That was months ago.

CLEMENT: Yes: And most of the change we see in him is due to you. You have cared for him faithfully and devotedly. Without you, I fear his mind would have been lost; and without that, he were better dead.

JOAN: And now, Clement? And now…..?

CLEMENT: I cannot tell.

JOAN: When he sees that the tomb has gone — and by my orders — how will it make him feel towards me?

*(CLEMENT is silent. Then JOAN speaks in a small voice, as if she had suddenly become a frightened child.)*

What will he do to me?

CLEMENT: Do to you? He might do anything —

*(He stops as WARE enters R. He is obviously better, happier and more in possession of himself than he has been yet.)*

WARE: I am going down to the Chapel. Will you come with me, Joan?

JOAN: No, my lord. If it pleases you, I would rather wait here.

WARE: How long is it since I have seen Nicola's resting place? I must resume my daily visits.

JOAN: *(In a strained voice)* Yes, my lord.

WARE: Now that the masons have finished their work at last, I hope they have satisfied you, Joan?

JOAN: They have satisfied me. I wonder if they could have possibly satisfied *you*?

WARE: I fear I have left far too much to your direction these last months, Joan. I have been an unsatisfactory master, and a sick man. But that is over now, and I take up my responsibilities once more. I am ashamed to think how heavily they have been falling on you.

JOAN: Indeed, I have not found them heavy. Anything I can

do is a light task, if it is of service to you.

WARE: *(Kindly, taking her hands)* You have been very good to me, Joan. I am deep in your debt.

JOAN: I am well rewarded, only to see you recover.

WARE: *(Turning to exit, back)* So — you won't come?

JOAN: No...I will wait. Oh! Come back quickly...and tell me what you think.

WARE: If I do not think it satisfactory, it will be my own fault, for having left too much to you — as usual. *(Smiles)*

JOAN: I shall be afraid — till you come back.

WARE: Afraid! I've never know you afraid of anything yet! *(He almost laughs, as he turns away, and goes out R. JOAN clasps and unclasps her hands in anguish and moves restlessly about.)*

JOAN: What will he do to me, Clement? — Do you think he'll send me away?

CLEMENT: *(Holding another little phial up against the light)* I shouldn't think so.

JOAN: Put that phial down! I want your attention. I want your help.

CLEMENT: I can do nothing till my lord comes back. *(Looking at the phial)* I believe I have the right proportions at last.

JOAN: I believe you're made of something different from flesh and blood! Phials! now!

CLEMENT: I must remind you, my lady, that without these precious liquids of mine, my lord would be a dead man by this time — in spite of your loving care.

JOAN: Yes, yes. But he's alive, and so am I, and we're not safe yet. Clement, why do you think he won't send me away?

CLEMENT: *(Absently, his fingers still on the phial)* Because you're too useful to him.

JOAN: *(Hurt)* Useful! Is that all?

CLEMENT: He has come to depend on you, and trust you.

JOAN: *(Sharply)* Put that phial where you can't see it!

CLEMENT: *(With the ghost of a smile)* I will put it where it cannot possibly exert any further fascination. *(Hides it out of sight)*

JOAN: Well, you know the truth, of course. I've never taken any pains to hide it, have I? I love my lord. I love him more than my own soul's safety.

CLEMENT: I must remind your ladyship that you are not free to love another than your husband.

JOAN: I was sold to Philip — ignominiously sold, by my father and brothers! It was not a marriage. It was a sordid bargain. They wanted Philip's money, that's all. They never cared about me.

CLEMENT: My lady —

JOAN: They gave me no love, so I gave them none back! And now, I hate them all for what they've done.

CLEMENT: To hate your own father and brothers is a grievous sin. It should be confessed and purged out of the soul.

JOAN: One of these days you'll drive me to be a Lutheran!

CLEMENT: God forbid!

JOAN: But He *didn't* forbid Luther, or our own Reformers! He didn't even forbid Thomas Cromwell to break up the monasteries, hang the Abbots, and steal their money for the King.

CLEMENT: *(horrified)* Hush! What are you saying?

JOAN: *(well away)* Added to which, we've had a Protestant Queen, and I, for one, am sorry she died.

CLEMENT: A judgement on her that she did.

JOAN: She lived long enough to give the King an heir, anyway. So who knows what we shall see in the future? And you! Godforbidding it won't stop the changes coming.

CLEMENT: You are much too ready to express yourself on matters that are beyond you. I beg to remind your ladyship that you are a subject and a woman —

JOAN: And therefore, a pawn in the game, like all women. We're married off merely for questions of dowry, and policy, and state. It sickens me. And it sickens me more that God's church and God's priests are content to bless such shameless marriages.

CLEMENT: It is a rule that the individual must be sacrificed for the good of the whole. I see no wrong in that. The Community is above the individual. Royal marriages, and marriages between people of rank and estate, cannot always be arranged according to the whim of the human heart.

JOAN: The whim! And suppose that whim is — love? Must the heart then betray itself, and see its love come to the dust of death?

CLEMENT: That, in any case, is the end of all earthly love.

JOAN: Oh, Clement, Clement! You ought to have been a priest! God should have forbidden the King's men to turn anyone like you out of a monastery.

CLEMENT: In the monastery, or out of it, I have made my vows. And the vows hold, , as far as I am concerned.

JOAN: But *I* have made no vows.

CLEMENT: Your pardon, Lady Joan, but you have. You made your marriage vows. They hold you, as surely as my vows hold me. *(He turns away with an air of finality.* JOAN *begins to fidget restlessly again.)*

JOAN: He's a long time, Clement. I can't bear this suspense. Perhaps he's ill...perhaps the shock has been too much for him. Have I done right? Tell me, have I done right, after all?

CLEMENT: A few minutes ago that point of view did not appear to be important to you.

JOAN: *(Twisting her hands)* Oh, can't you be human, Clement? There's nothing of the nun about *me*.

CLEMENT: So I observe.

JOAN: No — I'm not the renouncing, meditating, prayerful, obedient type. I've hated and I've been hard and unforgiving. But never to him — never to him. And I've only hated those who hurt him.

CLEMENT: And — you.

JOAN: That seems indistinguishable. Can't you understand?

CLEMENT: Understanding belongs to God. It is sufficient for man to obey.

JOAN: Go, go....My lord might need you, and that's all I can think of now. Go quietly, and see what he is doing.
*(CLEMENT prepares to depart.)*

JOAN: *(pacing)* Give me something to do till you come back.
*(CLEMENT offers his Rosary)*
No, no! Not that! My thoughts are not in heaven, they're on earth, *Brother* Clement!

CLEMENT: Then I cannot help you. *(Moves to exit R.)*

JOAN: *(who has subsided on the window seat)* Oh! *(Her hand touches a little packet. She picks it up.)*

CLEMENT: I observe that my young lord, your husband, still thinks of you.

JOAN: I wish he didn't! Still, he has the grace not to write me letters. Sometimes — I think there's a change of heart in him. These are some old Provencal songs and poems that he copied and translated for me.

CLEMENT: From his boyhood up, he has always loved poetry and music — like you.

*(He goes out. JOAN turns the pages restlessly)*

JOAN: Yes, this is the best.

*(With an effort, she concentrates, and reads)*

"I hold him but a fool, who makes alliance with love.

The more one trust it, the more unhappy one is.

One thinks to warm one's hands at the fire of love.

And one is scorched and burned.

The gifts of love come late, its miseries come every day,

Fools, traitors, deceivers, they are in the company of love —

Never have I gained so much, as when I lost my Beloved,

In losing her, I gained myself whom I had lost."

*(WARE comes in, and stands listening as JOAN reads the last two lines)*

WARE: Joan *(She gives a start and rises to her feet, dropping the parchment.)*

WARE: Read those last two lines again, Joan.

JOAN: I — I need not read them. They are in my mind.

*(repeats)*

"Never have I gained so much as when I lost my Beloved.

In losing her, I gained myself whom I had lost."

WARE: Yes....you have them in mind, I see....And now, Joan, what have you done?

JOAN: You have seen for yourself — what has been taken away.

WARE: *(trying to keep his voice steady)* Nicola's tomb...well? You were entrusted with its decoration and preservation. You have broken that trust. You have lied to me, and deceived me. How dare you do it?

JOAN: My lord, my lord, I have *not* deceived you —

WARE: How? Not deceived me? Will you add insolence to what you've done? We live in an age of desecration. All over the country tombs and shrines are despoiled and destroyed. Even the tombs of the saints are not secure. Nicola was a Saint, — far beyond your understanding — you, it seems are a despoiler and a destroyer.

JOAN: No, no, my lord, I am not! True, it was by my order,

and my order alone, that the tomb was taken away —

WARE: You dare to tell me this! You amaze me!

JOAN: I have stranger things to tell, if you can hear them.

WARE: More deceptions?

JOAN: I beg you will hear me out... Nicola is not, and never has been, buried in your private chapel...

*(WARE sways a little on his feet and involuntarily puts a hand to his head)*

WARE: *(muttering)* The shadows are beginning to creep back across my brain...God keep me in the light...

*(JOAN darts to his side instinctively, as if to give him support, but he pushes her away.)*

WARE: *(with an effort)* Well? Continue.

JOAN: That night you thought her dead, she did not die. Only her love for you — died.

WARE: How dare you say it!

JOAN: Because I dare to say the truth! Because I seem to be the only one in this cursed and crumbling house who does dare to say it! But you won't dare to listen. You prefer the shifting shadows to the clear light of day. You hide in illusions and dreams, because you cannot face the facts. Nicola loved Philip.

*(WARE sways again and puts a hand against the wall as if to steady himself.)*

WARE: *(with a tremendous effort at self control)* Prove that.

JOAN: Willingly.

*(She goes over to the window seat and from her bag produces the little packet of faded parchment with the yellow hair attached. WARE has followed her slowly, like a man learning to walk after a long illness. JOAN, with her back to him undoes the silk which ties the parchment and keeps this and the hair in her hands. Then she turns, and gives the parchment to WARE. He reads, with trembling hands, trying to keep his mouth steady. JOAN faces up to him with determination.)*

WARE: *(Muttering)* Philip — Nicola — Philip —

*(He looks up suddenly and sees the yellow hair in JOAN's hands. A wild expression comes over his face.)*

WARE: *(almost with a scream)* Her yellow hair — her yellow hair! How dare you touch it! How dare you hold it in your hands! *(He makes a rush, as if to snatch it from her grasp.*

*Instinctively* JOAN *clutches it to her and then runs to the fire place.)*

JOAN: There's only one way to end it! Nicola's yellow hair shan't be between you and me for ever!

*(She drops it on the fire and watches it burn. Then she walks slowly back and faces up to* WARE *again.)*

JOAN: Can you forgive me — and live?

*(He has been standing as if petrified. Now he drops the parchment and covers his face with his hands. Suddenly he gives a half moan, half sob, and crumples up on the window seat. In a moment,* JOAN *is kneeling beside him.)*

JOAN: *(clinging to him.)* Don't hate me! Don't hate me! Love her if you must…love her still, though she hurt and betrayed you. But don't hate *me*! Don't send me away.

WARE: Nicola! I can't believe it. I'd sooner believe that you were a hard, unscrupulous woman.

JOAN: Never hard to *you*.

WARE: You're jealous of Nicola. That's how it is. Jealousy is a devil that stops at nothing. This is your jealous work… you hate Nicola.

JOAN: No, not now. I think — I've only loved too much.

WARE: *(straightening himself)* Well, Joan, this is a sorry business But I vowed I'd be the master of the house again and I will. I want yet more proof. Does anyone else know of this?

JOAN: Yes. Clement can confirm all I say.

WARE: Clement! Then call him in.

*(She goes to the door R, and calls "Clement". He enters and she returns to her position near* WARE)

JOAN: I have told my lord of the empty tomb, Clement. Will you tell him what we know of the facts that unhappy night when he thought Nicola died?

CLEMENT: It seems, my lord, that the Lady Nicola cherished an unlawful affection for your nephew.

WARE: *(coldly)* I have been informed of that.

CLEMENT: The Lady Nicola was unconscious, but she still lived. You thought her dead, and refused to look upon her face again. You shut yourself away —

JOAN: The temptation was too much for Philip. He gave out that she had died of a plague and that you had ordered instant burial. That night, his personal servant, heavily bribed, carried

Nicola away through the dark. Philip followed next day, after the sham interment..

*(WARE looks questioningly at CLEMENT)*

CLEMENT: I confirm all this, my lord. The Lady Nicola died — but we know not when. She is buried, perhaps in Provence. But certainly not here.

WARE: But you watched and prayed by her that night!

CLEMENT: No. I slept the heavy unnatural sleep of a drugged man. In the light of later experience, I know that now.

JOAN: When I found — that parchment in Nicola's room, I told Clement. Some instinct, stronger than reason, prompted me to do what I did.

WARE: *(hoarsely)* And what was that?

JOAN: I gave the hair to the mason who opened the vault, and told him — to make sure. Then we knew that Nicola was not there.

CLEMENT: We confronted Philip with our knowledge. By every word and look he confessed himself a guilty man.

WARE: But Philip — my brother's son! Nicola, my only light... By heaven, but heaven is unjust! Men are only required to die once, and to lose by death once. I have died twice, and I have lost Nicola — twice.

JOAN: *(kneeling beside him again)* But *you* live!

WARE: My father ordered a man to be hanged once, for stealing deer. The rope was old and rotten and it broke. I can remember how the poor wretch screamed. I was a boy then, and they made me watch. But my father said justice had been done and let the creature go. To have hanged him a second time would have been unthinkable. Is God less kind than my sinful, mortal, father?

*(He pauses for a moment and then puts his hand to his eyes.)*

WARE: The shadows are closing in —

JOAN: *(gripping him)* No, no, they shall *not*! *(Pleading)* My lord, my lord, say you don't hate me! Say it!

*(He says nothing. Her hands fall. A terrible fear in her voice)* You — can't — say it?

WARE: *(dully)* I don't hate you, Joan.

JOAN: You forgive me? You won't send me away?

*(Again, silence — the fear growing)* Then, you can't say that?

WARE: No, I can't say that. You have robbed me of Nicola,

even if your story is true.

CLEMENT: It *is* true, my lord.

WARE: Still, I am robbed; and you have done it. After all, you are Philip's wife. You shall go to him.

JOAN: *(hiding her face against him)* How can you, after all he's done! I'd only hate him again — and her. And what will become of you if I go away? You'll fall back again into the dark.

WARE: *You* have taken away the light.

JOAN: No, my lord, I've only taken away the candles, and the deceitful shadows that go with them. I've opened the doors and windows in this sorrowful house, *(Clutching him)* Let me stay!

*(He disengages her hands, gets up and walks away.)*

WARE: No, Joan, no. Whatever Philip has done, you *are* his wife. Therefore you cannot be mine.

JOAN: *(Still on her knees, crouching against the window seat)* You mean I *must* go to him?

WARE: I mean it. I cannot live here with my nephew's wife indefinitely. The house cannot peter out in such a miserable scandal as that.

JOAN: *(bitterly)* The house! The house! Are these decaying stones of so much more value than my living flesh and blood? Do you prefer their mildew or my youth?

CLEMENT: My lord is right.

JOAN: Yes! The individual must be sacrificed for the good of the whole, for this rotting old house, full of ghosts and tombs, for the State that steals money openly from God's Church, and slaughters His priests; for the King, who divorces his rightful wife that he may wed another, and then sends *her* to the block!

WARE: Silence!

CLEMENT. Beware of heresy and treason!

JOAN: How you all hate the truth, from the King down! Didn't Anne Boleyn die on Tower Hill, then? Didn't the King take her sister before he ever took her? So what about the King's marriage vows?

WARE: The King is the King — and you —

JOAN: A woman; and therefore a pawn in the game — *(She gets up)* So you want me to go to Philip. We parted with bitter

words. But there was more than words between us that night.
There was a knife; and as far as I am concerned, there still is.
I'd rather die, and I'd rather he died, than that we should
live as husband and wife. I will never go back.

WARE: Think what you're saying! If you do not go back to him
— what can you do — a woman, young, lovely, and alone?

JOAN: Alone! *(There is a wealth of meaning in the word. She
faces up to WARE again)* There's only one thing to do, if
I'm alone. The night you thought Nicola died, Philip made
Bertram fight him along that passage. Bertram was forced
against the window, and crashed through.

WARE: So that's what happened! I could never understand —
or believe — the story Bertram told about his fall.

JOAN: They fought about Nicola. Bertram knew.

WARE: He knew?

JOAN: Yes. And Bertram's dead, isn't he? The house claimed
him and now it's claiming me.
*(She rushes out, down the corridor. For a second, the men
stand as if paralysed, then start in hot pursuit, CLEMENT
leading.)*

WARE: *(shouting)* Get her Clement! Get her! For God's sake
stop her! She mustn't do it — *she musn't* ..... She's making
for the window.....stop her, Clement.
*(Their voices die away down the passage. There is a scream,
a crash, then silence. After a few seconds, CLEMENT's voice
can be heard.)*

CLEMENT: Margaret, Margaret! Come quickly!
*(After a short pause, WARE enters, carrying the limp form
of JOAN in his arms. He is followed by CLEMENT, whose
habitual composure is considerably shaken for once. WARE
lays JOAN very gently on the cushion of the window seat.
Her arms dangle helplessly to the ground.)*

WARE: Clement, if she's gone, I swear, before Heaven, I'll
follow her.

CLEMENT: Peace, my Lord, peace. This is no Christian talk.
*(He feels her pulse, and heart.)*
She — lives.

WARE: God be thanked for that! *(While CLEMENT is attending
to her)* Clement, I'm no better than a murderer....I drove
her to it. Blind, and selfish as I've been, like a beast in my

blindness. I've taken all, and given nothing. I've driven her, alone and desparate, to do a ghastly thing like this — *(He kneels beside her)*

CLEMENT: *(calling)* Margaret! Margaret!

MARGARET: I come! I come!

*(She hurries in, as fast as she can, bringing flagons of water and wine and goblets.)*

CLEMENT: Water — quickly — my phial —

*(He hurries across the room and finds the despised phial where he had hidden it. He pours out some water, empties the contents of the phial into it, then he hurries back to* JOAN. *Margaret is already there.)*

MARGARET: *(tearfully)* My lady! My dear, dear lady!

CLEMENT: *(shortly)* Lift her head up — so. (MARGARET *obeys. He manages to pour the liquid down* JOAN's *throat.)*

MARGARET: *(wailing)* She's cold!

CLEMENT: Of course she's cold. It's November.

MARGARET: Oh, say she'll live, Clement! Say she'll live!

CLEMENT: She'll live.

WARE: *(in anguish)* But how? Like Bertram? Oh, Clement! What have I done?

*(He buries his face against* JOAN's *dress)*

MARGARET: Whatever made her do such a dreadful thing? My dear lady!

WARE: I made her do it, Margaret.

MARGARET: You, my lord? But how —

WARE: I told her she must go back to Philip. I thought it best —

CLEMENT: Look — she stirs!

WARE: She moans. Clement, Clement, tell me she'll not follow Bertram any further! Oh, there's a curse upon this house, this Hall, this passage — and if I'd only listened to her, she would have lifted it! She was young and strong and full of life. I've been living on her, on all her care and devotion. I didn't realise it....I've been asleep and dreaming and only God knows how bad my dreams have been.

CLEMENT: She stirs again.

WARE: I feel like death beside her; like death, looking at life... Tell me she'll come back; not halt, or maimed, but as she was alive.

CLEMENT: *(who has been feeling her limbs)* She'll come back my lord.

WARE: *(insistently)* But how, Clement, how?

CLEMENT: I — cannot say.

WARE: *(bending over her)* Joan! Joan! Come back! I need you!
I can't live without you! If you cannot come to me, then I
must go to you.

*(JOAN moves again, opens her eyes, and looks at WARE)*

JOAN: I — am — coming.

*(She looks round — gradually full consciousness returns. She
is badly bruised and stunned, but nothing worse.)*

JOAN: *(raising her head a little)* Something brought me back.
What was it?

CLEMENT: The contents of this little phial, your ladyship
was pleased to despise a short while ago.

JOAN: *(with a faint smile)* Thank you, Clement. *(to WARE)*
You said you needed me?

WARE: I do need you, Joan. I didn't realise, till I thought I'd
lost you, how much I'd lived on you all these months. The
shadows are always coming to darken my brain, and creep
into my eyes. I'd been blind....but for all I've done in my
blindness, forgive me, Joan.

JOAN: There is nothing to forgive, my lord. It is only such a
little while since I was asking you to forgive me for something I'd done — something — *(She closes her eyes and her
head falls tiredly back on the cushions.)*

WARE: *(gripping her hands)* Joan — Joan — don't slip away from
me like that — come back —

MARGARET: There! There! Let the poor lady rest! And if I
might suggest it, my lord, I'd have that window blocked
up.

WARE: I will, Margaret, I will. It's a cursed spot. It's a miracle
she wasn't killed.

MARGARET: It was the apple trees that Bertram planted that
saved her. They've grown well all these years since he — since
he — since my lady ordered him to have an orchard planted
there. I never saw anyone who loved apple blossom as she
did.

WARE: *(who has been only half attending)* Who?

MARGARET: *(after a fraction of hesitation)* The Lady Nicola.
*(At NICOLA's name, JOAN opens her eyes, and looks steadily*

*at* WARE *Their glances meet.)*

JOAN: So — it was Nicola's orchard that saved me.

CLEMENT: *(matter of fact)* And er, — feminine attire. *(looking at* JOAN's *wide skirt)* It always breaks a fall. *(Then he stands back and looks at* JOAN *with professional interest, mixed with monastic disapproval)* You have committed a rash and impious act, my lady. Take care. God has been pleased to save you once. It does not follow that He will do so again.

*(This means that she is now out of danger)*

WARE: *(standing up)* It is only justice that *she* should be saved, who saved me.

*(*JOAN *manages to raise herself to a half-sitting position)*

JOAN: Then I have done all that is needful. If you, my lord, are safe, and the master of the house once more, you have no place for me. I was out of myself when I did — what I am now ashamed of. After the long strain, something seemed to snap in my brain.

CLEMENT: A frequent occurrence, especially among the young and undisciplined.

JOAN: The Church hasn't the monopoly of imposing discipline, Brother Clement. Sometimes, life can be even more severe. *(to* WARE*)* I'll go, my lord. I think it best, now I can think again. I see you cannot have your nephew's wife for mistress of the house any longer. Now you are able, you must rule — alone.

WARE: Alone! Oh, Joan, that word sounds like a knell!

JOAN: I think it was that word that drove me to do what I did... alone!

WARE: Oh, God! Is there any answer to this grim puzzle that we call life? What *is* the answer?

JOAN: I will go back to my father. He still lives.

*(*HUGH *enters)*

HUGH: Your pardon, my lord, but the messenger grows impatient.

WARE: What messenger?

MARGARET: *(with a start)* Why, I had forgotten. A messenger came, spent with riding. He brought a letter and important news. I told them to get refreshment for him —

HUGH: He is, by now, well refreshed.

MARGARET: And just at the moment, my lady crashed...

you called for me…I could think of nothing else. My dear, dear lady! I thought she was dead. *(Starts to cry)*

JOAN: There, there, Margaret. I'm not dead!

WARE: Stifle that noise, Margaret. Give me the letter — give me the message — or whatever there is for me.

*(HUGH standing nervously in the doorway, beckons to MARGARET and gives her a letter. Then he whispers to her. It is evident that he has something badly on his mind,)*

WARE: Stop whispering, you fool! What's the matter with you? Speak out!

HUGH: Oh, if you please my lord, I daren't! I cannot do it. No, indeed, I cannot do it. *(He bolts from sight)*

WARE: Well, there goes a brave man-at-arms! Can you supply the missing information, Margaret?

MARGARET: Yes, my lord. Here is the letter.

*(She crosses to JOAN and gives the letter to WARE)*

WARE: This is an unknown hand — and the letter is for you, not me.

JOAN: I entreat you, my lord, break the seal and read it. *(To MARGARET)* Well, Margaret, I'd rather know what else fate has in store for me.

MARGARET: It is this — my young lord, your husband — is dead.

WARE: Dead!

*(JOAN falls back and buries her face in the cushions MARGARET puts a comforting arm round her. WARE composing himself with an effort, moves to her side.)*

WARE: Joan —

MARGARET: Read, my lord. She's listening.

*(WARE gives a preliminary glance over the letter)*

WARE: He must have dictated this. Yes, I see his name is signed at the end. You wish me to read it to you, Joan?

*(JOAN nods and WARE proceeds)*

"I returned to find Provence a desert, and the unhappy people exhausted by famine, fever and plague. Everywhere there is bloodshed, violence and suffering.

The armies of the Emperor Charles have been forced to retreat and I trust they have gone for ever. But, in pursuit, I have received a mortal wound. None may return to Provence and live. I could do no less than help defend the beautiful country

I love so much; yet I fear the defence was vain, for all round me is despoilation. I am in bitter pain and this moves me to confession, while there is yet time. How pleased Clement will be when he hears! I always guessed that old age would have none of me; and now I confess to all I was charged with the night I left you. Nicola only survived the journey to the South; she lies in Provence, where you, Joan would never come. Nicola is at home; and you, rightly, have stayed where your home will always be.

As for me, my destiny has made me homeless, in body and in spirit. Perhaps a new age will come, in which I might have found myself. I do not know.

Justice has been done, because I love you still.

Philip."

CLEMENT: May he rest in peace!

MARGARET: Amen.

WARE: I must speak to the messenger. Go, Margaret, and tell him the letter has been delivered and I am coming. Then return and see to her ladyship.

MARGARET: Yes, my lord. *(She gives* JOAN *a few motherly pats and goes.)*

*(*CLEMENT *experiences one of his rare moments of tact)*

CLEMENT: I, also would speak with the messenger, and Father John.....I hope he made a good end.

WARE: I hope he did not live to suffer long — he was born to be gay.

CLEMENT: I will return to her ladyship shortly. *(He moves to* JOAN's *side)* You are a brave woman, my lady Joan. And if it is of any satisfaction to you to know it, I think you have done right.

JOAN: *(who still has her face turned away into the cushion)* What did you say, Clement?

CLEMENT: It was not important, to you, my lady.

*(He actually smiles to himself as he goes out.* WARE *comes slowly towards* JOAN *and kneels beside her.)*

WARE: Joan.

JOAN: My lord?

*(Suddenly she buries her face against the cushions and gives a sob)*

WARE: Was that for *him*, after all?

JOAN: A little. *(She moves her hands and touches the books and papers that always lie close to, or on, the window seat.)* His books — his music — his Provencal songs — it never ought to have ended like this. I never belonged to him or to Provence. I always belonged *here*. He knew it, in the end.

WARE: Yes. And I know now that Nicola belonged to Provence, to the gay south, where I saw her first, drenched in sun. I was too old, too sad for her. I should never have transplanted her to this country of cloud and mist. Are you sure..... you don't hate her?

JOAN: I tell you again, I don't hate anyone — not Philip, or Nicola. I did once, but not now.

WARE: Nor I — not even now.

JOAN: Can't we have done with hate? There's a strange, new age coming. Can't we belong — to the future?

WARE: Joan, once again I feel I have been let out of a dark prison to look at the world, just as I did years ago in Rome when they let me out — and I saw — I met —

JOAN: I know. And you have been in prison again since, — the prison of your own mind — the worst prison of all. No strength of body can break those invisible bars!

WARE: But *you* broke them, and brought me out!

JOAN: Oh, my lord, my lord! This ought to be April, not November. It ought to be Easter Day, not the feast of Holy Souls.

WARE: Why, Joan?

JOAN: Because we live, in spite of everything; In spite of bloodshed, and war, and destruction round us everywhere.

WARE: "And yet I live". Do you remember when I found you reading that one April evening — was it months ago, or years?

JOAN: Life — wins.

WARE: And only a little while ago, death seemed triumphant. His wings were over you this very night. There seemed nothing stronger than death in all the world.

JOAN: *(winding her arms round him)* There is one thing stronger but only one!

CURTAIN

# LIGHTING PLOT

## Prologue. Autumn Evening in 1529

To open, the main source of light is from a small spot concentrated on a tall, ecclesiastical type candle, in a tall stand, which is up stage L.

There is an amber and red glow from the huge log fire down L. sending flickering shadows on the opposite wall. The misty evening light, which deepens during the scene, comes through the window L.C. and the bigger recessed window up L.

The corridor C is lit from off R. And there is an amber light outside the door down R.

1st. Change....Warning: 'Bertram' calls for lights "Hugh, lights here!"

Cue: 'Hugh' brings on two lighted candle brackets, from door down R. The overall lighting increases, sufficiently for practical visibility.

2nd Change....Warning: 'Margaret' "But she's past his aid now."

Cue: Hugh removes the lighted candles...and the general stage lighting decreases correspondingly.

For 'Curtain' to the scene, faint Blue at Windows up L.....
Fire Glow from fire down L. and light beyond door down R. And light in the corridor C.

## ACT I. Scene I. Spring Day in 1537

Full up lighting at rise of curtain, and throughout the scene.
Fire down L. and light behind door down R.
No lighting changes.

## ACT I. Scene II. Early Summer Day 1537

Late afternoon lighting to open. The lighting very slowly fades throughout the scene to a summer twilight.

1st Change....(The 'Burning down of the Monastery' off L.)
Warning: Bertram "Well, which do you think you'd prefer?"
Cue: (Bertram at window up L.) "What's that?...Over there... Do you see...? (A dull red glow becomes apparent, off L.) This rapidly increases to a full flame effect, in amber and red, which, rises and falls, and rises again, sending strange shadows on the room walls.

2nd. Change.....(The fire begins to die down...while the day-

light continues to fade)
Warning: Entrance of Lord of Ware and Hugh (Page 4)
Cue: Ware "of course you must stay here"...The fire off L.
begins to die down — but a faint amber-red glow remains outside windows, up L. until the end of the scene.

### ACT II. Early Summer 1537
(Afternoon lighting to open)

Fire down L...outside door down R...Lighting in corridor.
1st Change: Very slow 'fade' to twilight (summer) by end of
scene.
Warning: Joan "I hate you when you talk like that."
Cue: Philip "Oh, so you've found out about that, have you?"
('Outside' lighting begins to 'fade' very slowly.)
2nd. Change: As the daylight 'fades' in the room and corridor,
the 'blue' at the windows up L. decreases, while the 'glow' from
the fire down L. increases.
Warning: Joan "I accuse you of stealing my Lord your uncle's
wife by sickening treachery"
Cue: Joan "And where is she now?"
3rd. Change: Full twilight and firelight to end of scene.
Warning: Philip "What do you mean? You can't make me."
Cue: Philip "And would you want me to do penance after that?"

### ACT III. Late Autumn day in 1537

Full UP stage lighting...lighting in corridor...from fire down L.
With light outside door down R.
Lighting Change: A pale shaft of sunlight through window up L.
which illuminates Joan and Ware at end of Act.
Warning: Joan "Can't we have done with hate? There is a strange
new age coming....."
Cue: Joan "There is one thing stronger — but only one."
A shaft of pale sunshine illuminates Joan and Ware, followed by
a slow Curtain.

### Lighting effects. Off Stage

Prologue...Page 11...Shadows of the two fighters (Bertram and
Philip) are cast on wall of corridor C. (coming from R.) with
clash of steel on steel.

Warning: Philip "I'll make you sorry for that, you interfering hound."

Cue: As their bodies disappear along corridor to R, their shadows appear on the corridor wall…and 'duelling' sounds are heard. This is followed by 'glass crash' off R. So that the same 'warning' serves for both effects.

## ACT I. Scene II.

Shouts and cries off L. accompanied by sounds of the burning of the Monastery…'Crackles, and falling masonry'

Warning: Bertram "By my faith…It's the Abbey…Look".

Cue: Bertram "It can't be — They couldn't do it — No —"

Shouts — Cries — and General fire noises are intermittently heard from off L. These gradually die down as fire decreases. (Pages 2 to 4)

Sliding Panel up R. behind Tapestry.

Warning: Bertram "She has grieved for you…"

Cue: Ware "Pull it back, Bertram" (Panel opens to down stage)

Closing of Panel. (Pages 4 and 5)

Warning: Hugh "Yes, Sir. They know you're here……"

Cue: Philip "….Only remember that I loved you…" (Close panel)

Hammering on Castle doors, off R. together with shouts.

Warning: Ware "….Yes, but you'll follow him, of course…"

Cue: Joan "Yes, he must" (Shouts and hammerig on doors off R. These continue to end of scene. Pages 6 - 7 and 8)

## ACT III 'Glass Crash' off R. of corridor C.

Warning: Joan "There's only one thing to do, if I'm alone"

Cue: Ware "She's making for the window…Stop her, Clement!"

Tills Printers, Macclesfield.